ALPHABET CITY
my so-called sitcom life

ALPHABET CITY
my so-called sitcom life

Jon Paul Buchmeyer

Copyright © 2009 by Jon Paul Buchmeyer

All rights reserved, no portion of this book may be reproduced in any fashion, print facsimile, or electronic, or by any method yet to be developed, without express permission of the copyright holder.

Published by Buchmeyer Communications, Inc.

Printed in the United States of America

First edition, first printing

ISBN 978-0-9826112-0-3

For further information:
Buchmeyer Communications, Inc.
119 West 23rd St, Suite 401
New York, NY 10011
www.abcityblog.com

Cover designed by Samuel Griffin
All photos provided by author

*For Chef,
who provided sustenance in so many ways,
allowing me to pursue my dream.*

Viewer Programming Note:

Telling the stories of my life through the lens of a sitcom is my own personal coping mechanism. As such, some of the plot points have been punched up for comic effect, and some characters and guest stars have been exaggerated for improved ratings.

Contents

Episode 1	It Is Heavy	1
Episode 2	Will He Make It After All?	9
Episode 3	Summering	19
Episode 4	And Nothing but the Truth	29
Episode 5	The Bodyguard	37
Episode 6	Sex in the City	45
Episode 7	Turkey Trouble	53
Episode 8	As Bees in Honey Drown	65
Episode 9	Finger Lickin' Good	73
Episode 10	Blonde Ambition	83
Episode 11	Bold Faced Names	93
Episode 12	Even Jesus Needed a Publicist	101
Episode 13	Babylon	109
Episode 14	Happy Soul	117
Episode 15	And Baby Makes Three	127
Episode 16	Boots	135
Episode 17	Turn the World on With A Smile	139
Episode 18	Acknowledgments	149

Episode 1

It Is Heavy

Series Premiere. Learning the celebrity publicity ropes, Jon Paul battles an Oscar-winner's deranged cat. Guest star: Whoopi Goldberg.

From my post on a comfy love seat in Whoopi's study, I was straining to hear the conversation next door. The sliding doors to the living room were slightly ajar so I could listen to her interview with a journalist from a London daily who was barely audible. Brits are always so subtle, I thought. I inched down the couch closer to the door, surveying the titles of all the books crammed into the floor-to-ceiling shelves. Would she let me borrow *Midnight in the Garden of Good and Evil*? Still couldn't hear anything, so I tiptoed towards the door, when a twinkling golden light struck me, blinding me for a few moments. Dazed, I glanced high up on the shelf, and there it was, gleaming in the sunlight—the bald-headed beacon of artistic triumph. It was Whoopi's Oscar for *Ghost*.

I stopped moving. I stopped breathing. I'd never seen a real one before. I stood mesmerized, looking up at one of the most idolized statuettes in our civilization, shining down on me, demanding worship. My mind cranked into overdrive. Could the award possibly be as heavy as they say? Flashbacks of me as a kid, running around the backyard of our Texas ranch-style home, holding our blue Persian cat Pfeffa close to my chest as a furry stand-in for Oscar, thanking my parents and agent for the award. Laughing, crying, pausing, chuckling, leaning into the microphone—wow, this thing is heavy! Every winner says they're so heavy. Could it possibly be true? What's the harm of finding out?

I glanced over to the sliding doors. Whoopi was chuckling. The interview was going fine. I'd just pick it up for a few seconds and put it right back. Who would know? Hopefully not my boss.

In 1997, through a series of magical Manhattan coincidences, a Los Angeles-based entertainment agency surprisingly entrusted me—a 28 year-old Texas transplant living in New York City for less than a year—

to be their sole representative on the East Coast. I was struggling to master the skills required to be a celebrity publicist—a job for which I had no formal training. Each week, my duties were explained long distance by my boss who had a reputation as the nicest and busiest celebrity publicist in the business.

"Just sit in the next room while the interview is taking place. Whoopi wants the reporters to feel comfortable. So you'll be nearby," my boss said.

"Nearby doing what?"

"Taking notes. Listening in."

"Eavesdropping? I've been great at that since I was a kid. Some people say it's my super power."

"Relax. Whoopi's wonderful. You can't screw this up."

That night, on the eve of my Whoopi encounter, my best friend and roommate Angela—think hair of Minnie Driver with the determination of Abigail Adams—found me rifling through storage boxes stuffed into our East Village apartment's basement. My foofy little Bichon Frise dog Winnie wagged her tail anxiously at Angela, glad reinforcements had arrived to calm down the crazy train. Angela scooped up some old photos of me as a child actor in a community theater production of *Alice in Wonderland.*

"What's going on down here?" she asked.

"Oh my god, I'm meeting Whoopi tomorrow. I need to find this screenplay."

"Slow down. Why so nervous?"

"Because it's Whoopi! I have always adored Whoopi—loved her in *Color Purple, Ghost, Sister Act,* even *Sister Act 2.*"

"*Sister Act 2*? That is love."

Other than my dog, Angela knew me better, and longer, than anyone in the Big Apple. We became close friends at the University of Texas, both of us history majors sharing a love of Lady Bird Johnson and Princess Diana. A few years after graduation, Angela used her Democratic connections to land a spot at a New York City political consulting firm, and we became roommates when I moved to Manhattan.

I waved a 150-page masterpiece held together with gold brads.

"Here it is! The first screenplay I ever wrote for Whoopi. *Mrs. Claus*! A Christmas blockbuster."

"Whoopi as Santa's wife? I'd go see that," Angela said.

"Unfortunately, you don't run a studio. It won some minor writing awards, but never went anywhere."

Screenwriting was just one of my many disappointing career adventures I was trying to leave behind in Texas.

"How is it you're meeting with Whoopi about your screenplay?"

"I'm not, actually. I'm supposed to go to her apartment while some journalist interviews her. It's called 'covering.'"

She flipped through the first few pages of *Mrs. Claus*.

"Why don't you just see how it goes, first? Leave the screenplay pitch to later."

That night, with Winnie curled up by my side, I re-read *Mrs. Claus* and laughed—at the audacity of a middle class white kid from Texas thinking I could channel Whoopi's special blend of humor.

The next day, under the watchful eye of a doorman in a classy gray uniform and top hat, I paced nervously in front of Whoopi's Art Deco building on Manhattan's Upper East Side. Only two miles from my home in the East Village and I felt like I needed a passport to cross the border of 59th street into the wealthiest zip code in America. Downtown in my 'hood, the sidewalks were broken with giant cracks and dotted brown from ground-in dog poop. Uptown, the sidewalks were marble-like smooth and polished to a glistening white. The doorman only allowed me access once I handed over some identification. He mumbled a cryptic code into a phone, then nodded and directed me towards the elegant wooden and brass elevator in the rear of the lobby.

Just as I was readjusting my bag and wiping the sweat off my forehead, reviewing my game plan for faking my way through this task and planning what to say when I knocked on the apartment door, the elevator opened and I was deposited directly into the home's vestibule. Suddenly, and with no preparation, no time to gather my thoughts, I was standing face to face with the famously wide, toothy grin and dreadlocked hair that I had worshipped since I was a teenager. My Southern manners took hold and I stuck out my hand.

"I'm Jon Paul."

"I certainly hope so, or security is going to pot in this building. I'm Whoopi. Come on in."

She escorted me into the living room.

"Anything to drink?"

"Shot of vodka?"

She didn't laugh. I winced.

"Just kidding. Water would be great."

She went to the kitchen herself. I was impressed, no servants hovering nearby to do her bidding.

"How long have you been doing this?" Whoopi called out.

She returned and handed me the water, motioning for me to sit on the living room couch.

"Oh, not long, really. And you?"

"How long have I been doing this? Long enough. Have to leave next week for some backwoods Eastern European film set for a bad Disney TV movie—that evil mouse has me in an iron-clad contract."

She sighed heavily. I grimaced in sympathy and added a little shrug for effect—like I was under the same Mickey Mouse tyrannical rule.

"Traveling must be fun, though."

"I hate flying. Deathly afraid of it. Heavily medicate myself just to get on the Concorde."

"Wow, so fancy. What do you do when you have to go to LA?"

"I have a rock and roll tour bus loaded with books from Barnes and Noble. I read the whole way and love it."

I should give her *Mrs. Claus* for her next trip. We continued chatting like two girlfriends catching up, and I was smitten. Perhaps she would invite me onboard the bus and we could have our own book club.

"Where are you living?" she asked.

"In the East Village. On 5th street and Avenue A."

She smiled and nodded knowingly.

"Alphabet City, eh? Haven't been there in years. It used to be crazy down there. How's it now?"

The wailing of a deranged and mangy cat running along the back of the sofa interrupted our easy banter. Meowreowwwreowwreoww! I jumped up. Whoopi shook her head.

"That's just Pepper. I adopted her after she survived a horrible fire in Queens. See?"

She picked up a copy of the *New York Post* featuring a story of the rescued kitten and mention of Whoopi's adoption. I wondered if she might consider adopting East Village orphans like Winnie and me. Pepper was a sad creature with portions of exposed skin.

"She's getting used to her new home. A little skittish. Right, Pepper?"

I could have sworn the cat flashed me an evil grin.

A few minutes later, the reporter arrived and I shuffled off to the study, readying myself to "cover" Whoopi's interview. I was so nervous from the moment I arrived that it was the first time I had a chance to catch my breath and check out Whoopi's home. With light streaming in on all sides, accenting a boldly colorful collection of African-American folk art, I was mesmerized by how effortlessly beautiful the apartment was. It was warmer and more comfortable than the fancy New York homes I had glimpsed in the pages of *Architectural Digest*.

I settled on the little couch, and struggled to hear the questioning in the next room. I slid closer to the door when high on the bookshelves one of her most prized decorations distracted me. I found myself staring up at the first real Academy Award I had ever seen. It was just barely out of my reach—inches really. Should I get a chair? No, relax. I could do this. Up on my toes, I stretched as far as possible, fingertips just gripping the bottom edges of the statue.

A blood curdling ferocious feline scream from mangy cat Pepper surprised me. Meowreowwwreowwreoww! Pepper jumped onto my head from a hiding place nearby just as I was picking up the award. Meowreowwwreowwreoww! Pepper sunk her claws into my head. I struggled to maintain my grasp on Oscar. Meowreowwwreowwreoww! My scalp began tingling. I grabbed my head to soothe the pain, swatting at the fur ball with one hand, clutching the statue in the other. Wow, the thing was heavy.

Meowreowwwreowwreoww! Pepper dug her claws deeper into my hair. Unable to keep quiet, I let out a blood-curdling scream. Aaaarrrrgghhh! Pepper refused to give up. I needed both hands free to swat her away. And so, reluctantly, I loosened my five-finger grip on immortality, freeing the golden god, grimacing as he fell to the ground. Thunk! The statue landed with a loud thud, bounced one time, and then laid flat—a casualty of the battle with Pepper. The deranged feline jumped off my head and scampered away. Silence.

My screaming stopped. Whoopi's interview stopped. I stood there looking at the Oscar at my feet, mortified, knowing I was out of a job—banned for life from the Dorothy Chandler Pavilion. An interminable pause, and then Whoopi called out in a calm, measured voice.

"Everything okay in there?"

Paralyzed, I was unable to muster any sort of reply. I just stood there sweating and looking down at Oscar. Mercifully, after a few moments, the interview quietly resumed. I was in complete panic mode and my mind began racing.

Is there any way she didn't hear me drop the Oscar? From the sound, it probably ruined the hardwood floors. Oh God, is there any sign of injury to Oscar? I picked it up and examined him closely. Maybe a slight knick, but I couldn't tell as sweat dripped onto the shiny torso. Think. Think. Think. Wait, what if I snuck Oscar out in my bag? That could work. I could search online for some minor Oscar that someone was selling. On that site I keep reading about, eBay. One for Sound Editing, maybe. That might work. Then what? Sneak back in. Switch it out. A little *I Love Lucy*. A little complicated. But worth a shot. Shit, where's that damn cat?

Silence from next door. The interview had ended and I heard footsteps and small talk as Whoopi escorted the reporter to the elevator. I stood frozen, clutching her Oscar. Trying desperately to breathe. Trying desperately to summon a smile. Trying desperately to call up courage. The doors slid open and Whoopi looked at me pathetically, watching me caress her priceless statuette.

She crossed towards me gingerly—as if I were a crazed criminal brandishing a deadly weapon. Whoopi, cast as the SWAT leader come to reason me out of this dangerous situation, eased in closely, her dreadlocks just glancing my shoulder. She rested her hands on the Oscar, brushing my fingertips, and gave it a little tug. I loosened my grip, and let it slip from my grasp. The priceless golden body of immortal fame was safely in her possession again. Pepper trotted through, purring, and smirking.

I stood nervously, unable to move, turning blue from holding my breathe, watching Whoopi's back as she effortlessly replaced the statue on the shelf, positioning it just so. She turned back to me and smiled with that mouthy enveloping grin.

"Heavy, isn't it?"

Escorting me to the elevator, she gave me a reassuring hug.

"Listen, kid. Good luck. Take care down there in Alphabet City. You're gonna be fine."

I exhaled all the way home, making a mental note never to forget the grace and compassion Whoopi showed that day. She was like a guest star that had just put in an Emmy-caliber performance in an episode of my life. And my time in New York was turning out to be more sitcom than drama. What a relief. After years of toiling as a child in what I thought of as a prime time legal soap opera—think *L.A. Law* meets *Dallas*—I had escaped to Manhattan in my late '20s to explore a set of happier storylines. It looked like my so-called sitcom life even had a name—*Alphabet City*. Had a certain ring to it.

Next on Alphabet City*:*

Jon Paul's dream of living in New York doesn't come easily. "This will be the biggest mistake of your life."

Episode 2

Will He Make It After All?

After escaping the pain of Texas, Jon Paul uses Southern charm to defeat Japanese Power Rangers in the Big Apple.

No surprise really that I process my life through the lens of sitcoms and drama series considering that much of my worldview was formed by a steady diet of 70's TV programs and variety shows. Television was an event in my household—an opportunity for the clan to gather round the Sony TV in our ultra mod yellow and green den decorated with LeRoy Neiman tennis player lithographs. Instead of imparting pearls of wisdom around the family dinner table, my father used television as a way to instill morals and values. Every Sunday, when the TV guide insert came out in the paper, my father went through it with a highlighter—our cue as to what TV show lessons were on tap for that week. As such, he set the agenda—and the dial—with favorites like *Barney Miller*; *Welcome Back, Kotter*; *Soap*; and, my enduring role model, *Mary Tyler Moore*.

As a seven year-old, I spent an inordinate amount of timing thinking and worrying about Mary Richards.

"Will she ever have a steady boyfriend?" I asked my 16 year-old sister Pam.

"Mary doesn't need a man to be fulfilled, Paul, that's the entire point of the show," she replied exasperated. Her feminist streak, now fully developed, had emerged when she was two.

"Will Mary ever move into her own house?" I asked my 14-year old sister Paige kicking the soccer ball around our half-acre backyard.

"Nah, her apartment's pretty fab," she said, proud of the orange shag carpet in the bedroom she shared with Pam.

"Will we ever meet Mary's mom?" I asked my own mother who was unpacking a bucket of Kentucky Fried Chicken for dinner.

"Mary's pretty independent. She has a nice group of friends. You should have some friends like her," she counseled, always worried that I played mostly by myself.

"Where does Mary get her clothes?" I asked my constant feline companion Pfeffa.

"From someone named Evan Picone," I verbalized for the cat, reading off the designer's name from the closing credits.

"Will Mary ever get promoted?" I worriedly asked my father at dinner one night.

He was hidden behind the afternoon edition of the *Dallas Times Herald*, a dying breed of liberal journalism in Texas, and for the most part didn't engage in conversation with the family at dinnertime.

"Dad, did you hear me? Will Mary ever get promoted?"

Dad knew a lot about work because he was always there. He peered over the top of the paper.

"You'll just have to keep watching."

Week after week, year after year, Mary Richards, her friends and co-workers in the WJM newsroom formed the foundations of my perspective on life. Mary taught me that things work out in the end—just remember to have on a cute outfit when they do. She became my role model—perfect job, funny friends, and—after her move to the big city—no interaction with her family.

When Mary's sassy sidekick Rhoda Morgenstern got her own show and moved to New York City, I dreamed right along, plotting my life in the Big Apple. Maybe one day I could land my own series, leave behind my family and escape the long shadow of my father.

Dad was a larger-than-life character—a workaholic lawyer turned famously liberal federal judge, with a love of racquet sports like tennis and squash. He led a completely self-absorbed existence as the star of his own prime time drama, what I call *Courtside Manner*. With a detached demeanor and sarcastic wit, Jerry Buchmeyer was *Lou Grant* meets *Bob Newhart* minus any hint of their tenderness. *Courtside Manner* featured lots of legal intrigue and on-court lessons, with me appearing only occasionally in a small role. The star of the show was undeniably Dad, and I was merely a distraction.

Ensconced in a successful legal practice, he was out of the house by 5am, returning after sundown. Hearing the roar of his rickety Porsche scream down the winding street towards our house, I would run the length of our ranch style home, attach myself to his leg and go for a ride all the way back to his study. Outside the door to his private retreat, he would shake me loose and disappear behind closed doors for hours.

I credit both my parents with instilling in me a love of the dramatic. My father took great pride in exposing his family to the modern productions of the Dallas Theater Center housed in a landmark building designed by Frank Lloyd Wright. When I was 11, he took the family to see *Equus*, a show about a teenager's sexual angst who, while nude on stage, acts out by blinding horses. My father just ignored the stares of shocked fellow patrons.

Meanwhile, my mother took the more age-appropriate step of enrolling me in after-school acting lessons that I adored. She often put to use her seamstress skills producing elaborate costumes for my well-received supporting roles such as baby Roo in *Winnie the Pooh* and Grumpy in *Snow White and the Seven Dwarves*. I still have the pleated kilt she labored over for my role as Mr. McLaren in *Brigadoon*.

When not tap dancing my way to stardom, I worked by my mother's side in a bakery she owned called Cookies, featuring mass-produced versions of her homespun recipes. My help was required for a favorite known as Thimble Cookies. The fussy French baker working for my mother became increasingly frustrated that his thumbs were too large to make the required indentation in the tiny balls of butter cookie dough. One day, he threw a pan of the ruined treats across the kitchen at my mother. Nonplussed, she pressed my tiny pre-teen thumbs into immediate service.

Courtside Manner took a dramatic turn in October 1979, when President Jimmy Carter appointed my father to be a United States District Judge for North Texas, and Dad quickly made a name for himself as an activist jurist that conservatives love to hate. He dragged Dallas kicking and screaming into the modern era with landmark decisions advancing civil liberties and fair access to public housing. In 1982, when I was 13, he handed down a celebrated and derided decision in a case known as *Baker v. Wade* declaring unconstitutional the Texas law criminalizing homosexual conduct in private. He was celebrated by gays and demonized by conservatives. For added drama, he made sure I was in the courtroom for the hearings, which left everyone—including the press—wondering if the judge's effeminate son had any impact on the decision. Not exactly the kind of attention a kid struggling with his sexuality relishes.

My father's rise to prominence as a powerful judge marked the end of my parents' relationship. After suffering my father's wily ways for 25 years, my mother had enough—one night she left a letter in his study telling him to move out, and then she disappeared for the next several days. That night when Dad returned from work, my sister Paige hugged me close on her bed as we heard Dad sigh heavily when he read Mom's note. Then we listened to the whine of the sports car engine as it sped away from our house. It hadn't occurred to him to check on us.

My storylines on *Courtside Manner* only became more confusing as my parents officially ended their marriage. When I was 14, a week after the divorce was final, my father took me to our legally mandated Wednesday night dinner. He chose the faux-pub chain restaurant Steak & Ale where he usually ignored me in favor of the afternoon newspaper. But this time, he nonchalantly announced that he had gotten remarried the previous weekend to a woman whom I had never met. I didn't even know he was dating. The following Wednesday, over another dinner at Steak & Ale, he nonchalantly announced that the woman he married was 5-months pregnant—I would soon have a little brother.

"We need your room for the nursery. You won't be able to spend the night anymore," he told me.

Meanwhile, my mother announced her own engagement to a man who I quickly realized was the complete opposite of my father: a pipe smoking, religious, former merchant marine who suffered from bouts of depression. She decided to sell the only home I had ever lived in and move to a much smaller prefabricated house in an unfamiliar suburb of the city near my tony private school. At the same time, she began creating a life for herself with her new husband at a country log cabin she called Chigger Ridge.

With my prospects for improved storylines on *Courtside Manner* dimming, it was no wonder that I dreamed of landing my own show in New York just like Rhoda. In the midst of all this chaos, I actually thought my big break came when my acting talents landed me a part as the villain in an original stage show titled *Calling All Kids*. It was a sickeningly sweet all-child musical review conceived by Tony Award-winning legend Tommy Tune's producer Phil Oesterman. When Tommy came to see the show in tryouts in Dallas, I just knew he was going to twirl me away from my misery and right onto the Great White Way, hopefully into a penthouse apartment with Central Park views.

Unfortunately, the reviews were brutal. The local paper called the show "half-baked" and said I was "chubby"—an eerie foreshadowing of my life-long battle with weight. After two shows a day for two weeks during Christmas break, I was so exhausted and depressed from my parents' shenanigans that I took to my bed like Scarlett O'Hara and stayed home from school for nearly a month.

Over the next year, I did everything a desperate 14 year-old could do to get attention—stole credit cards, stopped eating, lied incessantly, cheated on tests, smoked pot and began having lots of sex with my best friend. Despite all my efforts, neither parent paid much attention. When I turned 15, teachers finally raised the red flag that I was failing school, possibly anorexic and desperately in need of guidance. My father begrudgingly allowed me to come live with him and his new family, and my mother stopped speaking to me for months.

Through the rest of high school, my father continued to ignore me for the most part, communicating through a series of post-it notes and expense checks left on the kitchen table. By then, I decided that my best shot at landing my own show in New York was attending Columbia University. I buckled down, turned my grades around, got noticed as a nationally ranked debater, and graduated near the top of my class. With the help of my school advisors, I earned early admission to the school of my dreams. Finally, it was all coming together—I would be escaping Texas and my family and going Ivy League! But my plan was crushed in a way I never anticipated. My father left on the kitchen table a small post-it note attached to my acceptance packet.

"I will only pay for state school."

Suddenly, there would be no Columbia, only his alma mater the University of Texas. Devastated, I summoned up the courage to ask him face-to-face why he even let me apply to Columbia—he had to sign the application after all, so he knew how much it cost all along. Why not just tell me upfront about his imposed financial limits? Why even let me raise my hopes?

"In a million years I never imagined you would be accepted," he answered.

My final season on *Courtside Manner* came when I was a sophomore in college. My father, who never visited me at school or inquired as to what I was studying, called to tell me he was cutting me off. Never a financial wizard, he claimed money was tight with his new family. He also took the opportunity to tell me that I wasn't welcome to come home with my boyfriend. My stepmother worried that my little brother would turn gay being around us, and my Dad felt it was his duty to support her. Never mind that Dad was a hero to many in the gay community and knew better. He had never taken my side—I had always been a burden. And now he was through with me. I had been written out of his show.

His betrayal drew me further into the arms of Nathan, a cherub-faced boy from Midland, Texas and we moved in together when I was 19—practically getting married as a teenager. I got a job, took time off from school, and then took out some hefty loans to finish my degree. Nathan was a drifter and I supported him financially through a non-stop set of career changes—from library science to massage therapy—while he tried to find what might make him happy. After five rocky years, Nathan and I struck a deal that he would work and support me while I followed my newly adopted dream—filmmaking.

On a lark, my oldest sister Pam and I had begun writing screenplays together. Screenwriting quickly became an all-consuming escapist fantasy akin to dreaming of what to do with winnings from a Powerball Lottery. We spent hours concocting ways an imagined screenplay sale of $1 million would solve my student loan and credit card debt.

One year later with several unsold scripts for Whoopi and another few for Meg Ryan, we tired of waiting for Hollywood to discover us and I was bored with graduate school. In an amazing show of hubris, we decided to take matters into our own hands and film an independent movie. It never dawned on us that neither of us had any true experience. In 1995, everyone with a credit card could be an auteur—indie films were the new garage bands! Why go to film school when we could learn on the job? Within five weeks, we cranked out a script for a comedy ensemble called *GayTV: The Movie*, and in six months secured enough money to begin shooting on a shoestring budget.

A week before principal photography—after raising nearly $300,000 from investors, leveraging our credit cards, casting 17 actors in the ensemble, and hiring a talented crew to manage the work—Nathan broke our agreement. He quit his job and announced he was leaving me and moving to San Francisco.

"Watching your dream come true is too painful for me," he said.

I was stunned, but had to shake off the betrayal and get down to work—there were nearly a hundred people counting on me to keep it together, stay focused and complete filming. When the four weeks of intensive shooting ended and my adopted family of cast and crew faded away, I was left to cope with normal post-project depression compounded by the death of my failed relationship. I was out of money with no one to support me emotionally or financially.

Prospects for the film were mediocre at best—distributors didn't know what to make of a big gay comedy filled with parodies of pop-culture TV hits like *Charlie's Post-Op Angels*.

"Are you willing to reshoot? Because I can only market movies with AIDS or hot gay sex," said one clueless hetero-executive.

I walked out of those distribution talks, and closed the door on any possibility of wide release. While *GayTV: The Movie* was accepted into some B-list gay film festivals in Turin and Philadelphia, I could see that my career as an indie film director was headed nowhere fast, and that my life had crumbled into a complicated disaster. My indie comeback was not working out as planned.

A life preserver appeared in a new friend, Jimmy, a blond-haired country boy who drove a truck and listened to a little too much Debbie Gibson—think two-stepping feet of Garth Brooks with the puppy love smile of Donnie Osmond. He was a professional therapist and could sense I needed support. To battle my depression, he forced me out of bed every morning and drove me to breakfast. Our talks over coffee and huevos rancheros at the local gay diner Lucky's convinced me that to heal my soul I had to leave the pain behind.

"Time for you to move on. Reinvent yourself somewhere else," Jimmy advised.

"Well, I've always wanted to live in New York. But starting over again just seems so daunting. Finding a home, a job, friends, love."

"You're a survivor. Things will work out."

I took a sip of coffee and thought maybe he was right. Things always worked out for Mary Richards. Could I follow in her footsteps? Just thinking about my 70s TV icon started melting away all my worries about moving to New York. Sure, I was older than the typical college kid moving to the city fresh after graduation. Sure, I had no clear idea about what job or apartment or boyfriend I might be able to find. But the same was true for Mary. She left behind a jilted fiancé, started fresh in a new town, and survived by discovering the bright side of almost any situation.

So at 27, moving to New York from Texas in 1996, I calmed my nerves by telling myself I was escaping the dramatic storylines of my youth. I was finally starring in my own gay boy version of the *Mary Tyler Moore* show. Just like when Mary passed the Minneapolis sign on some midwestern highway, the catchy theme song *Love Is All*

Around played as my internal camera panned from my overloaded U-haul to the "New York City, Holland Tunnel" sign.

Just like when Mary first arrived and battled Rhoda over an insanely well-designed apartment, I had a similar fight over my first NYC home—only not with my best friend. In my sitcom set-up, my pal from college, Angela, and I joined forces and battled a group of Japanese Power Rangers. The East Village apartment we desired was in a newly renovated building, and while it was slightly more than we could afford, it had two levels, and a backyard, perfect for my foofy dog Winnie who was accustomed to carousing in her own grassy yard in Texas.

Only thing standing between us and our new sitcom set were seven Japanese kids who had just graduated from high school, dressed head-to-toe in colored leotards with matching helmets, and flashing a wad of cash. Their parents were willing to pay the entire year's rent up front. It was an offer that John the Greek landlord, just venturing into the realm of NYC real estate, could hardly refuse. Our shot at a fabulous pad was slipping away.

But if there's one thing I learned from Mary, it was a little charm goes a long way. We invited the landlord to lunch—he looked like a guy who didn't miss a meal. Over latkes and applesauce at Leshko's Polish Diner just down the block, Angela and I asked John about his family. He beamed as he showed us wallet-size pics of the strapping young men.

"It's a very big Greek family. All my sons in the business with me."

"Well, I can't wait to meet them," I said, wondering if any of them were single.

"Must be so wonderful with them being so close for you to look after them," Angela added.

"It's so hard for us moving to New York from Texas, so far from our families," I chimed in.

I looked away out the window—like I was about to cry, when actually I was about to burst out laughing at the lie I was telling. While Angela was certainly close to her family, my father's parting words echoed in my head, "This will be the biggest mistake of your life."

I turned back to the landlord and went for the close, ready to pick up the check, intending to pay with money I had borrowed for the apartment's security deposit. I leaned in, looking him squarely in the eyes.

"John, let's be honest, after all the blood, sweat and tears you put into that amazing apartment, who would you rather have in there? Two good kids from Texas that are going to care for the place like a real home? Or the hard-partying Power Rangers who will trash it in a year?"

While thinking about the cash the Asian superheroes were flashing, John looked at Angela, then at me—my eyes pleading with him for a break. He smiled.

"Alright, you will have apartment. Welcome to Alphabet City."

After dreaming about this moment for over 20 years, I grabbed the keys to my first New York apartment—and the beginning to a new sitcom life in the Big Apple.

Next on Alphabet City:

Jon Paul gets hit on by his new boss. "Relax, we're just getting started."

Episode 3

Summering

With a little help from Mary, Jon Paul lands a new job in the Big Apple.

Three weeks after moving into my East Village apartment, I tried settling into my new life in Manhattan that was turning out to be soggy and expensive. It seemed like the April rains would never end, and unanticipated taxes were shrinking my already measly paycheck. Thankfully, my trusty *TimeOut NYC* guide had suggestions for low-cost entertainment and pointed me to a nondescript building struggling to make a name for itself sandwiched between its much taller brethren on West 52nd street. The Museum of Television & Radio archived almost all television shows in history—including my Holy Grail, the most important series ever to plant itself firmly in the imagination of a fey boy growing up in the wilds of Dallas.

My free entertainment and escape from the madcap life of the city that never sleeps was watching the first episode of *MTM* in the museum archives just a few blocks away from my dreary temp job. It was before TiVo's and DVR's, and the whole rudimentary playback technology fascinated me. Every lunch hour I had the same routine: shake off the rain and march confidently up to the counter. The portly librarian with hair pulled back in an up-do and a "Relive the Moments" button on her jacket always rolled her eyes at the sight of me.

"I'm here to see Mary Tyler Moore," I announced.

As always, I handed to the librarian a slip of paper with my selection—the first episode of *MTM*. She assigned me a cubby, and a few minutes later, as if by magic, Mary, Phyllis, Rhoda, Lou appeared on my monitor—they were my reliable companions and trusted guides to life.

Just like *MTM*, my sitcom life had lovable friends and a great apartment set, but it was missing the glamorous job. I was getting by working for test prep giant Kaplan and was drowning in a depressing soup of acronyms—ACT, SAT, GRE, GMAT. The problem was that I wasn't sure what I was qualified to do. Most of my life I wandered from interest to interest relying on my brains and good attitude to get by. While that worked well in famously slacker Austin, New York seemed to require more focused ambition, something my father had once informed me I lacked.

One late night over pierogies at Leshko's, our now go-to *Seinfeld* diner, Angela gave me a job-hunting lecture.

"Listen, it's all about connections. I work for a connected lady who has more clients than she can handle. And I can't handle all the work by myself."

She sipped her coffee, and I noticed a tiny cockroach running under the ketchup bottle and looked the other way. Roaches were bigger in Texas.

"I think it would be fun working together. Don't you?" Angela asked.

I sipped the bitter coffee—a cup o' joe was soothing in Texas but here it was my pick-me-up drug of choice; I counted on it giving me the necessary jolt of energy for surviving this hectic town.

"I'm not really sure what you do. And your boss sounds crazy."

"She's dramatic. It's public relations. What do you expect?"

Angela motioned for the check—discussion closed.

A week later, I was at the East 53rd Street upscale Italian hang out San Pietro sipping my first-ever glass of Pinot Grigio at an outside table, enjoying the oncoming slight chill of an early summer afternoon. Women teetering on impossibly high patent leather pumps rushed by with oversized dark brown shopping bags from the Gucci flagship store nearby. I was keeping a lookout for its chief designer and sex symbol Tom Ford during my job interview with Angela's boss Madame—think sophistication of Candice Bergen with the sex drive of Candace Bushnell. This whole scene was more like the city of my dreams than my dreary Kaplan desk blocks away.

"That's Charles over there. We dated for a while. You know him, right?" Madame asked.

She waved her too-tanned arm with Cartier tennis bracelet and matching diamond rings at the too-tanned Charles across the line-up of packed-in bistro tables. I shook my head "no." Madame sighed.

"Well he controls the most important economic development agency around. You have to go through him to get anything done in this town. Appointed by the governor, also a friend, of course."

She repositioned the cream-colored summer cashmere sweater around her shoulders. We never wore sweaters past March in Texas.

"Hello Al! See you next week! Aren't you looking younger than ever?"

Madame waved suggestively at an older wrinkly Italian gentleman with thinning hair. I shuddered; he was far from alluring yet Madame was acting like a sex kitten in heat. Angela piped up.

"That's Senator Alfonse D'Amato. We're organizing a fundraiser for him next week. You should come."

"Over my dead Democratic body," I laughed.

Madame took a gulp of wine, staring me down through her Jackie O. sunglasses, not amused. Angela chimed in to cut the tension.

"Jon Paul's Dad is a federal judge in Texas. Appointed by Carter. Jon Paul knows Democrats inside and out."

She was stretching the truth, and I flinched at the mention of my Dad. He was powerful, but had never run for office in his life, which meant that other than Ann Richards, I couldn't name another Texas Democratic politician. But Angela knew how to publicize my credentials.

"I think Jon Paul would be perfect as a press person for our favorite client."

Angela flashed me a grin. I smiled back. Madame took another sip of wine, basking in the fading sun, tired of being hounded.

"Fine. He's hired. Anything to keep Angela happy."

Miraculously, I had just landed a new job in the world of public relations—an industry I knew little about. Madame interrupted my reverie.

"Get some appropriate clothes and pack your bags. We'll be summering in The Vineyard."

Until I moved to the Big Apple, I had never heard the word "summer" used as a verb. But from what I could tell, the entire society stratus of New York City greeted summer with a mass exodus. For those that could afford it, summering meant scheduling into two-day weekends all the things we took for granted on a weekly basis in Texas—swimming, tanning, boating, golfing. The perfect New Yorker recipe for summering was taking your already hectic life of the city—drinking, shopping, eating, cruising—exporting it to a seashore community along with everyone you know from your life in New York, adding a few outdoorsy extra curricular activities, mixing in some sand, commuting traffic, and then stirring it all up into a frenzied madness.

Summering ensnared all kinds—Fags to Fire Island, Snobs to Southampton, Monied to Martha's Vineyard. New Yorkers returned after Labor Day bronzed and exhausted. In Dallas, we just went to Lake Texhoma and returned leathery and pickled.

Summering for my family meant returning to the piney woods of East Texas to visit my grandmother in her mobile home trailer next to a Dairy Queen and a catfish pond. I was just one half step removed from white trash. But in Texas, practically everyone was in the same boat so it wasn't until I moved to New York that I began to feel embarrassed by my Southern roots. I had never experienced the expansive wealth that seemed endemic to New York, but my new job with Angela was giving me a crash course in the summering habits of the rich and famous.

After just two weeks of answering Madame's phones, which I was instructed to answer in a breathy and annoyed voice, I found myself sweating nervously into the powder blue leather seats on the private jet of the firm's biggest client. Billionaire—think charm of Steve Guttenberg with the ears of Michael Eisner—was playing flight attendant on the short flight to Martha's Vineyard. He smiled as he handed me a crystal tumbler filled with soda.

"Here's the Diet Coke you ordered. Didn't my Mom do a nice job redecorating the plane?" Billionaire asked.

"It's really something. I'm used to Southwest Airlines," I said.

He stared blankly, trying to connect to someone on the other end of the wealth continuum.

"I think I own stock in Southwest," he offered.

When Billionaire returned to the galley, I stared out the jet's window. Billionaire's efforts to make me feel comfortable just accentuated how out-of-place I felt in the midst of so much conspicuous consumption. And as we touched down smoothly on the island famous as a summer playground for the powerful, I wondered how I had replaced Heather Locklear as Sammy Jo on a Northeastern version of *Dynasty*.

Unlike the Hamptons just a highway hop from Manhattan, Martha's Vineyard maintains its exclusivity because it is hard to get to. If you aren't one of the privileged several hundred with a private jet, you have to drive through the winding roads of the Massachusetts Cape and make sure to book a slot on a ferry crossing several months in advance. Even with a jet, you might find yourself suffering landing slots at unfriendly hours and enduring several minutes in traffic on the small runway as air traffic controllers struggled to avoid collisions of Boston's wealthiest with New York's most powerful.

The inviting charm of Martha's Vineyard—the Cape Cod cottages, the gingerbread village, Edgartown's white mansions built on the backs of whales—is punctuated by constant reminders that outsiders aren't welcome. As we drove down one road clogged with black SUVs, Angela pointed to a gate.

"That's where the Clintons stay. They borrow someone's home. They're Southerners like us, I'm not sure they're allowed to buy."

Despite the constant reminders of social status, I found something quietly peaceful and reassuring about the summering citizens of The Vineyard. A sense of camaraderie. A collective sigh of relief, "Whew, we made it. Now let's buckle down and kayak!" You might not have been invited to the latest Democratic fundraiser down the street, but you'll get over it by taking in the sea breeze on a beach walk past the dramatic cliffs of Gay Head. Who knows, you might even spot a Kennedy, or three.

At the Chilmark General Store, Angela and I rustled up the necessary ingredients for the down home hors d'oeuvres we were serving that evening to Billionaire.

"You still think pigs 'n a blanket is the way to go?" I asked.

Billionaire's food issues made me nervous about his announced desire to try pigs 'n a blanket when we arrived at The Vineyard at our boss Madame's summerhouse. He had a fear of eating meals prepared in someone else's kitchen. Restaurants were fine, but dinner parties at people's homes were frightening. This posed a huge problem in his society world with a packed schedule of "summering" with friends in The Vineyard.

"Trust me, always a crowd pleaser. He'll love them. Little effort, big results," Angela replied.

She grabbed some ready-to-bake Pillsbury crescent dough and a $7 can of Vienna sausages, and we were in business.

That night, the smell of freshly baked pre-packaged bread with a hint of fried bologna overwhelmed the odor of pinecone potpourri at Madame's house. When Billionaire arrived, Madame sneered at us in the kitchen.

"He's not going to eat that, you know. He never eats anything at someone else's house. Let alone something out of a can."

Angela spiced up the pigs 'n a blanket display with the addition of honey mustard to the usual dipping sauce of ketchup. She smiled as she placed the tray down in front of Billionaire. He studied them for a moment, then plopped a naked one in his mouth.

"Oh wow…hmmmm."

Billionaire chewed and swallowed. Madame gulped some wine. There was a pregnant pause.

"I've never tasted anything quite like this. Could we take some with us to the party?"

Over the next two weeks, Angela and I made at least seven-dozen batches of pigs 'n a blanket that Billionaire took to and ate at every party he attended. Turns out, a couple of Sammy Jo's from Texas could teach these Yankees a few tricks.

A month after the end of "summering," just when I thought I was getting the hang of my first real New York City job and perfecting my pissy PR voice, things turned ugly. Madame fired me on ethical grounds. I had them; she didn't.

It all started when she dispatched me to pick up a gown at the exclusive retailer Bergdorf's and pay for it with a credit card that Angela had warned me was only to be used for expenses on a particular client project. When I raised a concern, Madame lectured me.

"But this is a client expense. I have to look good on their behalf."

Later, I worried about the legality of organizing congressional candidate fundraising events sponsored by our client—a defense contractor with lucrative business dealings pending before his committee. When I raised another concern, Madame scolded me.

"This is the way business gets done in this state, get used to it."

Threatened by my willingness to confront her, Madame decided it was time for me to go. In her twisted mind, she created an outrageous scenario that gave her cause to fire me, accusing me of plotting to start a competing agency and steal her most lucrative client—Billionaire.

"I gave you a chance and you squandered it. Now get out."

There was no reasoning with her. So I grabbed my coat and left, and Angela quit in solidarity. We walked the forty blocks from Midtown back to the East Village, and I counted less than $30 to my name. Only six months in the Big Apple, and I'd managed to get myself fired. What exactly was I going to do now? Things were looking bleak, and I needed a pick-me-up.

The City Cinema on 2nd Avenue was playing *The Little Mermaid*. Just the thought of Ariel singing "Part of Your World" perked me up. So I bought us cheap tickets to the matinee, and settled in with all the other kids and nannies. Just before the lights dimmed, the work cell phone I forgot to leave behind began ringing. It was Billionaire calling. He probably hadn't heard the drama.

"Hi, I'm glad I got you. Heard the news. You're talented. You'll bounce back. And I've got an idea. A family friend is in town and I was hoping you'd entertain him. Take him out, show him the town, you know what I mean?"

I had witnessed Billionaire playing matchmaking yenta with his straight friends, and he knew I was gay, so I assumed that "entertain" must mean I was going on a date with this guy. Was he really setting me up when I had just been fired? Billionaire told me his friend's name, and I remembered he did public relations for Billionaire's brother, an Oscar-winning producer in Hollywood. Besides David Geffen, we were probably the only openly gay men Billionaire knew.

"He's a very good friend of the family, you'll like him. Take good care of him. Take really good care of him. I'll pay for it. You never know where it may lead."

The overuse of euphemisms made me feel a little dirty.

That night, I dragged my feet down West 44th Street and paused outside the uber trendy Royalton Hotel, where Billionaire's friend was staying. The models as doormen were dressed head-to-toe in form-fitting black outfits that probably cost more than my month's rent. They simultaneously yanked open the giant doors to the dimly lit lobby, and I felt like Alice through the looking glass—the chiseled bellboys with pearly white grins were Cheshire cats. I had never stepped foot in the Royalton before since I couldn't afford a drink there, much less own the appropriate wardrobe for lounging about on the overstuffed white lobby furniture. In Texas, fancy hotels came with soaring atrium lobbies and lots of green ferns, but this one was dark and gloomy with menacing minimalist arrangements of seven-foot high cherry blossoms. I spotted the house phone next to the front desk and called up to my date's room.

"Well hello, JP. The kid from Texas come to fetch me," Billionaire's friend boomed in a creepy singsong rhythm.

"Hey there. I'm downstairs and there's supposed to be a car for us. Should I just wait for you?"

"JP, why don't you come up and hang out for a while. I need to finish primping. How's that sound, JP?" he asked suggestively.

"Um, okay, sure."

But I wasn't sure about going to his room, or about the nickname he had created from my initials. No one had ever called me that. It felt too intimate.

The tiny elevator spat me out onto what I thought was the right floor. It was so dark I couldn't see anything and had to pat the walls with my hands as I walked down the dark hallway. I knocked on the door of what I hoped was his room, since I could barely make out the numbers. After a few moments, the door swung open and there in nothing but an open bathrobe stood Billionaire's friend Greasy—think heftiness of Will Ferrell with the nerdiness of Larry David.

"Care for a drag? I'm almost ready."

Greasy held out a joint. He was ready all right—for something more than I was prepared to put out. What had Billionaire told Greasy about this good time I was expected to show him?

"You know, why don't I wait down in the lobby?" I sheepishly replied.

"JP, JP, JP, what's the rush?"

Greasy ushered me in and told me he just needed to finish shaving.

"Have a drag while I finish up? Relax. We're just getting started."

His suite looked like an expensive porn set with slick wood paneling, mirror accents, and a sparse couch that on closer inspection had some unusual stains. Greasy dropped his robe in the glass walled bathroom that overlooked the suite's living room. I tried to look the other way as Greasy pranced about the room, smoking a joint, alternating between a robe, a towel, and his birthday suit. There wasn't an ounce of him I found particularly attractive. I interrupted the burlesque show.

"Not to be a pest, but we're going to be late for dinner," I said.

"What if we just ordered up some food, stayed in, talked, drank, smoked, you know?"

He winked, letting it all hang out. I stood up and headed towards what I thought was the door.

"Billionaire will be so disappointed tomorrow when I tell him you weren't able to go, especially after I used his name to get into the restaurant."

"I know Billionaire pretty well, JP. I'm sure he'd want us to have a good time."

"I'll meet you in the lobby in five if you're coming."

I pulled on a handle and, with a big flourish, walked right into the closet. Mary Richards would have been proud.

Dinner was in a new, much buzzed about Chelsea restaurant in a converted firehouse, and I spent much of the evening trying to douse Greasy's under-the-table advances.

"So tell me, JP, how's a Texas farm boy enjoying life in the big city?"

Greasy rubbed his foot up against my ankle.

"Oh, you know, it can be hard."

"I bet it can. Why don't you show me?"

His foot moved up my leg. I brushed it away. Needing reinforcements, I reached for the bottle of wine and Greasy put his hand over mine.

"Why don't you let me fill it up for you?" he asked lasciviously.

Greasy enjoyed getting me tongue-tied and flustered.

"I love making you blush."

On cue, I turned a bright shade of red. And then I got mad at myself. Why was I letting Greasy get to me? I needed to get a grip on myself—I learned about wrangling bucking broncos ogling cowboys at Rodeo Days. I straightened my spine in my best Mary Richards imitation.

"Listen up, Greasy. No more innuendos. No more touching. No more anything. You got that?"

He grinned.

"And another thing, no more calling me JP. My name's Jon Paul. You got that?"

"Well, well, well. There's the Texas spunk I'd been looking for."

He licked his lips. Disgusted, I made a move to leave.

"Sit down, JP. Oops, I mean Jon Paul. I've got a proposition."

I rolled my eyes.

"No, no, not that kind of proposition. I need someone to work for us in New York. The firm is growing. Clients are demanding. We need someone we can trust here. You've got this charming Texas innocence. I can tell you're a good kid. How about it?"

"I'll do it!"

Without asking any questions, and having no idea what the gig entailed—I signed up for a new job, just like Mary Richards did in her first interview with Lou. A few hours ago I was wandering the streets of New York and singing along with an animated mermaid. But now, just like Mary taught me, things seemed to be working out—and I even remembered to have on a cute outfit.

We climbed back into the car Billionaire had sent for the evening and headed back to Greasy's hotel. I watched the twinkling lights of Manhattan pass by dreamlike, in a blurred effect like I had seen in so many movies. Texas innocence? I had wasted so much energy trying to suppress parts of my Southern ways, that I missed how some of that charm and spirit could help me navigate the world of New York's power brokers. I turned back to Greasy.

"I don't understand exactly what it is you want me to do."

"Oh, my people will be in touch with details. You'll start with some celebrities—easy stuff—the same kind of thing you do for Billionaire."

"Maybe they'll like pigs 'n a blanket," I said.

The car pulled up in front of The Royalton. The doormen had added sculpted black topcoats to their ensemble.

"Want to come up?" Greasy asked.

"No, I'll pass."

"Good boy. You've got integrity. That's rare in this business. You're going to need that."

He rolled out of the car, winking at the doorman, and turned back.

"That, and a sense of humor."

"Lucky me, I've got that in spades."

Greasy had put me through the sexual innuendo ringer, and I had squeezed through to the other side. Things were happening to me; paths were opening up. I might still be an outsider in this New York world of jaded sensibility, but my sense of can-do spirit was blossoming and taking me places.

But nothing quite prepared this Texas wildflower for my entrance onto a much more glamorous and treacherous stage—an industry predicated on the promotion and protection of outrageous egos.

Next on Alphabet City:

Jon Paul doesn't quite know what to make of his latest client. "Get ready to have fun on the Tyra tour!"

Episode 4

And Nothing but the Truth

Jon Paul's vow of honesty lands him his biggest client. Guest stars: Tyra Banks, Cameron Diaz, Liza Minnelli.

Ignoring the stares of her fellow diners, a strikingly beautiful African-American woman in a wrap dress piled her plate high with delicacies from the Rhiga Royal's breakfast buffet. She grabbed muffins, waffles, and biscuits—trigger foods that would send most mortals to a Carbohydrates Anonymous meeting. I stood next to her scooping up some fruit and a little granola trying to stay committed to losing the Freshman 40 I had gained about 10 years ago in college. She reached across me for some bacon and smiled.

"I'm just one of those lucky people with a metabolism that lets me eat anything!"

Having all my life struggled with weight issues, I wanted to hit her. But I restrained myself because this supermodel could be my new client—if I passed this interview. She had final approval over who from my new firm would work with her. Some would have been nervous, but not me. It was 1997, well before any of us knew she would be America's Next Top Media Mogul, and I knew absolutely nothing about Tyra Banks.

For a few months now, I had been struggling to master the duties required to be a junior celebrity publicist. Other than a brief and almost disastrous encounter with Whoopi, so far my primary job had been escorting the firms C-list clients to be the third guest on NY-filmed TV talk shows like *Rosie*. These clients usually played the sitcom's whacky next-door neighbor but had a dramatic movie-of-the-week to promote. As a favor to the firm's heavy-hitter publicists who promised to deliver their headliners, talent bookers slotted in our low-wattage names in the last few minutes of a show.

Each week, my responsibilities were explained long distance by my boss, BusyB—think blonde highlights of Ryan Seacrest with the easy attitude of Neil Patrick Harris. He was Greasy's partner in the firm, headed up the celebrity division, and had a reputation as the nicest and busiest entertainment publicist in the business. BusyB was responsible for teaching me the public relations two-step dance I call "Spin and Cover."

First, I mastered the art of spin. A few days after my job interview-date with Greasy, BusyB called with my first assignment—a very important daily mission involving Liza Minnelli. By 7am, I was to read all the daily gossip columns, cut out and paste up any that mention Liza, and fax them to her manager, assistant and head publicist at 7:30am. No earlier or later.

Liza's entourage seemed awfully high maintenance, but that was fine by me. As cliché as it is for a gay boy, I have been completely devoted to Liza ever since I was six years old and my father took the family to The Venetian Room at Dallas' fading Fairmont Hotel for a live performance by the diva. It was the waning days of 70's hotel cabaret but I dressed as if it were the second coming.

For weeks, I pranced around the living room with a top hat and cane found in my stash of dress up clothes singing along to the cassette recording of *Cabaret*. I was perfecting a heart-wrenching rendition of "Maybe This Time." At Liza's performance, I quietly mouthed the words as I sat enraptured by her every word, note, gesture and sequin.

Twenty years later, I couldn't believe my good fortune to be traveling in her orbit. Which is why I was so unnerved when after a few weeks of successful gossip column faxing, BusyB assigned me a more critical Liza task.

"I need you to call Richard Johnson at *PageSix* and deny that Liza is back in rehab," he said.

"Richard? He's the most powerful columnist around. I've never spoken to him. Why me?"

"Because I've spoken to him a million times. He won't believe me."

"But I wouldn't even know what to say."

"Anything. Make something up. Like she's going into the hospital to have a procedure. Her knee or hip drained, something like that. It's called spin."

Spin sounded an awful like lying to me. Didn't Greasy say something about my integrity landing me the job? With no other options, I called Richard, but he wasn't buying what I was selling.

"You're honestly expecting me to believe some junior flack telling me that Liza is having her knee or hip drained?"

I paused, and then just tried to be as honest as I could.

"I know, but give a kid a break. I'm in over my head here, and my boss is telling me I have to feed you this story."

I could hear Richard typing away on his keyboard.

"That's the most honest thing I've heard all week," he said.

Next day, *PageSix* ran with the Liza-back-in-rehab story. But Richard included at the end of the piece an obscure line about Liza's reps claiming she was having a medical procedure. I was heralded a hero in the LA office. Greasy had told me the key to this business was keeping my integrity in tact, and surprisingly that is what charmed the most important gossip columnist.

Once I had spin down, BusyB introduced me to the next part of the celebrity publicist dance step.

"I need you to cover a shoot with Cameron this morning. Just show up and make sure they don't ask her to do anything she doesn't want to do," he announced.

"What, like pose nude?"

"I don't think you'll have to worry about that, it's for a teen magazine."

When I arrived at the stark white loft space in the still seedy Meatpacking District, a woman was waving around clothes on a hanger and shouted at me.

"Thank God you're here! Did you want to look at the selections? I've thrown out *so* many," the woman said.

Her crisp and clean starched white dress shirt indicated she actually hadn't been working too hard at throwing out anything. There looked to be close to 200 items still hanging on the multiple racks.

"A couple of pieces Cameron likes are off the shoulder, bare back. I've sent them back to Donna's folks to see about adding something."

"Who's Donna? Why no bare back?"

"Karan. Helps hide the blemishes."

Cameron Diaz's photo shoot was my introduction to being part of an entourage. Populating the loft were a collection of stylist characters—clothes stylists, hair stylists, make-up stylists, set stylists, food stylists, stylist stylists and more. Many of the stylists told me later they were Cameron's "go-to" people, which meant they had worked with the star before and were handpicked for this shoot. Given their closeness with Cameron, it seemed unlikely to me that anyone on the set would ask her to do anything uncomfortable.

Covering a photo shoot turned out to be one of the most boring things I've suffered through in my life. Close to thirty people hanging out on couches, drinking coffee listening to some unknown alternative rock bands. The only person missing was her boyfriend Matt, whom I had an enormous crush on, and I spent most of my time nervously wondering if he might show up. All that for a second rate teen mag.

Weeks later, after I had perfected the celebrity flack tap routine with Liza and Cameron, BusyB was ready to trust me with a much more important assignment. This could be my shot at moving up the rungs of entertainment publicity.

"One of my girl's needs someone a little more sophisticated to work with her. Last night, my other kid assigned to her got drunk at an awards show and rode around in her limo with the sunroof open, screaming," BusyB said.

"Got it. No acting like a frat boy, then. Who I am meeting? I'll die if it's Cher."

"We don't represent Cher. It's Tyra."

"Tie-who?"

"Tyra. Tyra Banks. Black supermodel."

"Oh, I don't know her."

"Don't have time to give you a full history. She's going on book tour and wants to approve the person I assign to her. I need you to make this work. Now she's very smart, very together. She's expecting you within the hour."

In the taxi on the way to the hotel, I gave myself a pep talk. I might not know anything about this Tyra, or what it meant to "go on book tour," but I needed to make this work. This was my chance at the big time.

After Tyra grazed the breakfast buffet, she got right down to business.

"Are you gay?"

I spit out the hotel's rich coffee and knocked over the dainty china cup. Now, I've never really hidden my sexuality, since I came out to my father and stepmother when I was 15 while eating Domino's pizza around the coffee table watching *Cheers*. But I was not accustomed to questions about my sexuality being the opening line of a job interview. She had a lot of nerve. But I couldn't imagine a supermodel surrounded by fag hair stylists and make-up artists could take issue with a gay publicist. The waiter rushed to mop up the mess, and I looked at Tyra confidently.

"Is my sexuality going to be a problem for you?"

"Of course not! A good gay is exactly what I'm looking for! Over the next couple of months, we'll be spending a lot of time together, in some tight situations, and I can't be worried about you."

Tyra touched my hand and smiled. She motioned down towards her voluptuous bosom and nodded at me knowingly. I stared at her blankly, not at all sure what she was getting at.

"Do you even know who I am?" she asked.

Now that's a question that can go either way with "famous" personalities. Mostly, it's the up-and-coming D-list celebrities who overestimate their worth and are offended by a lack of knowledge of their exploits. They're the kind of people who are always saying to club bouncers and airline gate agents, "Don't you know who I am?" I mean, if you have to ask, well then…

I took a sip of newly poured coffee and leaned in, knowing that this was a make it or break it moment.

"No, actually I don't know who you are."

Tyra knitted her brow, opened her mouth, but I continued.

"Here's the thing. I may not know everything you've done. But I'm an honest guy. I will always tell you the truth. Wouldn't you rather have that than some yes man always telling you what you want to hear?"

Tyra tilted her head, began to nod, and then smiled.

"Girl, we're going to get along just fine! Get ready to have fun on the Tyra Tour!"

She took a big bite of a bagel smothered in cream cheese, and I ate the last crumbs of granola, still jealous of her metabolism. She was a big presence all right—one that might just give a much-needed ratings boost to *Alphabet City*.

A few days after I passed my audition with Tyra, rolls of paper spewed forth from the fax machine recently installed in the firm's New York office, also known as the basement of my apartment. Winnie barked at the whirring sound and began biting and tearing at the pages coming through.

"Winnie stop! I need those!"

I chased her around the living room as she hopped from futon to futon, pleased that she had invented a new game. Angela arrived to offer assistance.

"What's going on down here?"

"Winnie stole my itinerary for Tyra's book tour!"

Winnie took one look at Angela and laid down, letting go of the fax. She knew who was in charge. We began piecing together the torn itinerary.

"I still can't believe you don't know who Tyra is. You never saw her on the cover of *Sports Illustrated*?"

"I don't read sports magazines, Ang."

"Come on, it was the swimsuit issue. You enjoy a good set of boobs."

She was right, even as a gay guy who idolized the male form, I had a healthy appreciation of the female bounty. Maybe it was envy.

"Well, I certainly didn't tell Tyra that in the interview. That's what she's worried about—some guy who can't take his eyes off her tits."

"Do you think they're real?"

From the file I had been reading in preparation for the book tour, there had been quite a bit of controversy over whether Tyra had been surgically enhanced.

"I don't know, but I intend to find out. I'm Nancy Drew and the case of the supermodel boobs."

Angela smiled and rubbed Winnie's tummy, taking a small bit of paper out of the dog's mouth and handing it to me.

From what I could surmise from the itinerary, we were traveling the country mostly to promote Tyra's book *Inside Out* on TV and in bookstores. In addition, we were also squeezing in appearances at Targets and Wal-Marts as part of her contract with CoverGirl. In each city, we would be busy from before dawn to well after midnight, then fly to the next city and start all over again. The night before the tour began, my boss offered more advice on the phone.

"Mostly, you'll be saying 'no' a lot. No Tyra won't appear on your show. No Tyra won't sign that. No Tyra doesn't have time to say hello. No Tyra doesn't want to take a picture of you with your teddy bear named Tyra."

"Oh, I get it. Kind of like being a bodyguard. I'm Kevin Costner to her Whitney Houston!"

"Um, right. Call me if you need anything," he said worriedly.

The one thing I needed was a copy of Tyra's book. Always the overly prepared student, I thought it important to have a thorough knowledge of the material before the teacher gave me a pop quiz. But no one was able to get me a copy—not our office in LA, not even the book publisher.

And now it was too late because my flight with Tyra left the next morning. I'd just have to come up with an excuse and tell Tyra my dog ate my homework—it was partly true. But I had a nagging feeling Tyra would know I was faking. And I couldn't afford to screw this up.

Next on Alphabet City*:*

Jon Paul comes face to face with a famous bosom. "Are Tyra's boobs real?"

Episode 5

The Bodyguard

Crisscrossing the country on book tour, Jon Paul gets real with his client. Guest star: Tyra Banks.

By the time Tyra and I arrived in Detroit—the last stop on the grueling month-long whistle-stop book tour—I should have learned enough to know that something was not right with this downtown "luxury" hotel. It was well after midnight, we were both exhausted, and I didn't realize how bad it was until Tyra called me from her suite.

"My room is unacceptable. There's a switch that vibrates the bed, and a Jacuzzi right next to it. I can't stay here," she said.

"Okay, so it's no Four Seasons. But let's just stay put for now. I'll look into options in the morning."

It had taken a while for Tyra and I to develop such an easy rapport. Like any traveling couple thrust into stressful situations, we quickly learned each other's quirks and requirements.

On our first flight together, I learned to appreciate Tyra's natural beauty. I was supposed to meet the supermodel-turned-author onboard Delta's flight from LaGuardia to Atlanta. But a woman I did not recognize was sitting in my seat 3A. The frumpy lady didn't have on a stitch of make-up—a sure sign they just let anyone fly first-class these days. I spoke to her in my best pissy voice.

"Excuse me, ma'am, I believe that's my seat."

"Oh, do you mind? I do much better by the window. Would you take my aisle seat, just this once?"

The interloper stared at me through her gold-rimmed glasses while smoothing back her ponytail. It took me a few seconds to realize the slightly ugly duckling pleading with me was Tyra.

"Um, sure. I mean I usually like the window. But whatever. I guess this time it's fine."

I decided it was best not to make an issue of it on our first trip together. Tyra smiled at me, put the hoodie up on her cashmere sweat jacket, turned to the window and fell immediately into a deep sleep.

After three glasses of bad cabernet sauvignon that was just good enough to calm my nerves, I stole Tyra's copy of her book stuffed in the seatback pocket. I was suspicious of a tome about teen self-esteem written by a supermodel—what exactly did a glamazon like Tyra have to say to all the ugly kids out there to make them feel better?

The first few pages of photos did nothing to dissuade me of my disdain for the book's concept—there was Tyra laying across a pool table all sexed up, there she was glammed up in African garb, another one of her staring amorously into the camera in stockinged feet. This was going to be a tough sell, not only to me, but also to the world it seemed.

I continued flipping through the pages, rolling my eyes at her tips for using eyeliner and performing at-home pedicures. Tyra stirred at the window, and turned facing me, still asleep. She didn't look so perfect. A little mole under her chin, dark circles under eyes, and was that a zit near her mouth? If only the public could see what I was seeing, that would give everyone a little self-esteem boost.

I continued paging through, and came upon an almost exact image of Tyra's imperfection reproduced in the book. There on page 60 was a picture of pre-makeup Tyra with handwritten annotations like a Sunday football play analysis. Circles and lines notated all the areas on Tyra's face that would need some serious work in order to make her look like the glamorous "after" photo on page 61. She really was putting it all out there for everyone to see. I held up the page with the before picture to the sleeping beauty Tyra next to me—just to get a real-life comparison. I took another sip of wine, and settled in to read about all of Tyra's other problem areas—legs, hips, forehead.

The demystifying of the beauty process fascinated me. As a young gay boy, I struggled mightily with the images of beauty forced upon me by my own community—chiseled chest, washboard abs, not an ounce of fat. No one was writing a book pointing out that it didn't just take hard work in the gym; it took blessed genes and a mountain of steroids to achieve that pumped up look. I made a note to give Tyra a suggestion for a follow-up book that I could help co-author.

Once the plane landed, the tour was a blur of on-the-job training:

In Atlanta, I learned the pre-dawn hours of hair and makeup were the last bit of calm before the onslaught of the day.

In DC, I learned to always carry an extra copy of Tyra's book along with a summary of key points and list of suggested questions because the host of the local "Wake Up" morning show will have lost hers.

In Philly, I learned to set a rule at Barnes & Nobles appearances that Tyra wouldn't autograph anything other than her book—not *Sports Illustrated* swimsuit covers, not Victoria's Secret bras.

In Boston, I learned to have on hand extra fat black sharpies for book signings because regular size pens cause hand cramps.

In Minneapolis, I learned that chips with the fat substitute Olestra cause Tyra to have intestinal distress.

In Cincinnati, I learned that teddy bears are a sure sign of craziness—anyone who shows up at a book signing offering a stuffed animal probably needs a security escort.

In Houston, I learned that the hotel concierge would helpfully pack up all the macramé sweaters and chocolates that fans give to Tyra along the way and send to a local homeless shelter or hospital.

In Dallas, I learned that Tyra thinks white limos are tacky.

In Chicago, I learned that Tyra had the skills to be a successful talk show host—on the way to O'Hare, I was caught in her confessional.

"Alright JP, let's hear it. When was your first time?"

"First time what?"

"Having sex, silly. You told me you've been out since you were a teen. So who was the lucky guy?"

A question like that coming from anyone else would have been shocking, but Tyra had a hypnotic affect that lured subjects into letting down their guard.

"Oh, it's kind of crazy actually. It was Halloween. I was 15 and dressed as a ladybug. He was a bumblebee."

"JP, learning the birds and the bees. Tell me more."

"The drama club had just put on a Halloween show for the little kids at our private school. We were still in our insect costumes, hanging out in the bucket seats of his Honda. One thing led to another. His bee stinger started growing. My ladybug wand came out swinging. And before I knew what was happening, I learned to drive stick shift."

"Oh JP, talk about trick or treating! So he was he your first love?"

"Yeah, but it ended tragically. He left me for a girl who was part of The Yellow Brick Road in our school's version of *The Wiz*."

"Girl, your school did *The Wiz*?"

"It was a semi-Jewish production. I was the Tin Man."

I curled up in a ball in the corner exhausted from the book tour and limo confessional. Had I really just revealed my first sexual encounter to my client? Tyra was busy changing her top. I acted like I wasn't looking.

"Can you reach in that bag and see if I have another bra in there?"

I handed her a new over-the-shoulder boulder holder, and she snapped on her extra-large Victoria's (not so) Secret. Looking out the window, we were passing by a park with lots of cute guys on the street, walking their dogs. I missed Winnie and the rest of my co-stars back in New York. But I would be home soon enough. Just one more night on the road. And I felt like I was finally getting the hang of the job. Plus, I had never been to Detroit. Motor City was the last stop on the Tyra Expressway. How bad could it be?

Normally, 5-star properties escorted Tyra directly to her suite, and let me handle all the check-in paper work. But our Detroit hotel was so excited about Tyra's arrival, that the front desk clerks, bellboys and assistant managers all wanted to have their pictures taken with her. While the flashbulbs popped, two burly gentlemen arrived in cheap suits—clearly inebriated with cocktails in hand. They begged and pleaded with Tyra to join them at their event in the hotel's ballroom.

"Tyra, love of my life, where have you been all night?" one said.

"We've been waiting for you. Why don't you come have a drink with us at our party in the ballroom?" the other slobbered.

Stupidly, I had let our security guy go for the evening. Tyra looked at me exasperated. Now a practiced pro at saying "no," I steeled the courage to explain to the former linebackers that Tyra wouldn't be attending their soiree. I puffed out my under-developed chest.

"Guys, it's not going to happen for you tonight."

They clenched their fists and started moving towards Tyra and me. I stood my ground, sure that I was about to get a playground pummeling from the bullies. I had lots of practice at this in grade school.

Tyra sensed an escalating situation, put a hand on my shoulder and pulled me aside so she was right up close to the drunken behemoths. She cocked her head and turned on the charm.

"Now ya'll, I gotta go up to my room. I've been going all day. But I might see ya'll later, okay? Be good."

And with that she stepped into the 80s atrium elevator and ascended to her Presidential Suite which she informed me later looked like a porn set. After I brokered an agreement with Tyra about finding a new hotel in the morning, I drifted off to sleep for about ten minutes. Then the phone by my bed starting ringing, and the voice on the other end was screaming.

"Those fools are outside my room—you've got to get me out of here," Tyra yelled.

The drunken salesmen downstairs had found out Tyra's room number, and this time weren't taking "no" for an answer. Now I was really in deep celebrity publicist shit, and I wasn't sure what to do. Pacing around the room, I pulled out the Yellow Pages. These were the days before everyone carried laptops and hotel rooms came internet equipped, so the phone book was my only resource. I flipped furiously through the hotel listings. Fuck! No Four Seasons. What else? What else? Ritz-Carlton Dearborn? I had no idea where that might be, but I dialed the number and asked to speak to the one person I had learned can get you out of tight situations—the hotel concierge.

"Hi, sorry to disturb you. I'm calling for Tyra Banks, we're in a little bit of a situation."

When I told him the name of the hotel, he cut me off.

"Say no more. It's being handled, Sir."

Within five minutes, he phoned me back, told me to take Tyra to the freight elevator at the end of the hall. He had a friend working there who would escort us down to the loading dock where a black SUV would be waiting to whisk her to the Ritz-Carlton. In the meantime, he was sending a white limo to the front as a distraction, with extra security to escort me and Tyra's luggage out of the building. We executed the decoy plot so expertly, I thought for a second I might have a shot at being a gay action-star sidekick.

The next morning, after loading up on carbs at the hotel's breakfast buffet, Tyra and I hustled through the final book tour appearances in Detroit, and both breathed a sigh of relief as we made one final connection in Chicago. We were parting ways as she headed back to Los Angeles, and I returned to New York. Our last trip together through O'Hare Hell was sure to be a special moment—it might be the last time I got to see my angel American Airlines Special Services Representative Lee.

An airline's special services staff member is the cousin of the hotel concierge saint—two people who can make a celebrity publicist's life run much smoother. You keep their numbers on speed dial, alert them to impending arrivals, send them gifts on every major holiday, and sometimes develop crushes on them.

We crossed paths with Lee several times on our multitudes of layovers in Chicago's unwieldy airport. His job was to meet us at our arriving gate in one of those fancy oversized golf carts with a candy-striped roof, whisk us to the Admirals Club, wait for us, and take us to our departing gate. Evidently, the idea is that a cart going two miles per hour discourages fans from accosting the famous faces inside. It's important for airlines to keep the celebrities happy so that whoever is sponsoring their tour keeps paying the full first class fare for them and the entourage. As a rule of thumb, celebrities don't pay for anything themselves if they can help it.

For our last meal together in the Windy City, Tyra had something special in mind. She directed our airport escort accordingly.

"Lee, honey, just drop us at McDonald's."

We were exhausted and hungry, and Tyra loved to eat. Lee looked over at me for approval. I winked—I loved a man in uniform.

"We'll be fine. Tyra's gate is just right over there," I told him.

I waved goodbye to Lee, as Tyra marched up to the mini-golden arches and ordered us both fries and cheeseburgers.

A huddled mass of people gathered around us at McDonald's, gawking at the site of a supermodel ordering America's favorite Happy Meal. As we moved towards her gate, the group of fans followed, and like a snowball slowly picking up mass as it rolled, the crowd grew and grew until we were surrounded at the gate.

Ignoring the mob scene, Tyra set up dinner shop on a couple of rickety gate side seats, chewing her fries, chomping the burger, and flipping through *Vogue*, not a care in the world. Just as I managed an exhausted bite of my sandwich, a woman stepped up.

"Tyra, can I take a picture with you eating fries?"

Tyra tuned her out. But I assumed my duties and spoke up.

"No, not right now, please. We're eating."

"Tyra will you sign my boarding pass?" shouted another.

Tyra ate another fry, flipped another page. I put down my burger.

"No, not at the moment, thank you."

The crowd started closing in, and I had to once again become the No-Sayer when all I wanted to do was eat like a normal person. Suffering sleep deprivation and hunger pains, I was more celebrity P-O-W than Kevin Costner Bodyguard. I looked down at my Whitney, sitting there oblivious to it all, dunking her fries in ketchup, and teared up, convinced I was about to collapse—my media tour life flashing before my eyes.

In the distance, above the shouting fans, I heard a faint sound. Beep. Beep. Beep. Beep. The group parted like the Red Sea. And there, through the crowd, came my White Knight, Lee, galloping to my rescue in a souped-up golf cart. He smiled at me, and patted his hand on the seat next to him. I leapt into the cart by his side, and reached my hand out to Tyra, who was blissfully savoring French fashion and fries.

"Ya'll go on. I'll stay here. These folks don't bother me. But girl, you need a break."

"Are you sure? I might not see you again. My flight leaves soon."

"You've done a great job. Now get out of here. Go spend time with your man. I have a feeling we'll see each other again. And that's the truth!"

With that, Lee threw the cart into reverse and motored out of there. He drove down the halls of O'Hare Hell and parked in a quiet corridor with a big window out to the tarmac. He smiled at his damsel in distress chowing down on dinner. I chewed and summoned up a smile, worried there might be a sesame seed stuck between my teeth. He leaned over and gave me a peck on the cheek.

"Can I ask you a question? Are Tyra's boobs real?"

It wasn't the first time someone had asked me this question on the tour. I had rehearsed a pretty good answer.

"Well, I've had the privilege of seeing them up close and personal. All I can say is that Tyra's bosom is something—and as far as I can tell, real."

As I silently watched the planes make their way down the runway, packed with business travelers and families as exhausted and hungry as me, I wondered about the unexpected plot turn *Alphabet City* had taken over the past several months. I sort of missed my traveling companion already.

Despite the exhausting and sometimes irritating nature of the book tour, my Tyra time was intoxicating. For a suburban Texas boy, the allure and glamour of it all was enticing—even if it wasn't quite what I expected when I moved to New York City several months earlier.

But as crazy as the ride with Tyra had been, I was ready to get home and tackle my next challenge—finding everlasting love.

Next on Alphabet City:

Jon Paul makes a fool out of himself at VH1's Divas Live. "I loved Coming out of the Dark!"

Episode 6

Sex in the City

Jon Paul becomes a Cosmo fan; then makes a pass at a pop-star's husband. Guest stars: Teri Hatcher, Gloria Estefan.

An unwelcome side effect of my travels with Tyra was the damper it put on my dating life. Other than a brief flirtation with an airline official at O'Hare, I rarely had the time to pursue a boyfriend, and that was beginning to depress me. Part of the appeal of moving to New York was an escape from the rigid structure of gay beauty in Dallas. Back there, everyone obsessed over the rugged football player type, and I was either overweight or dangerously skinny—other than a couple of minor bouts of anorexia in high school and college, I have always hovered about 23 or so pounds above my goal weight. Those extra pounds always made me self-conscious when standing in a gay bar surrounded by men with perfect abs.

In New York, there was a wider range of what constituted sexy—literally something for everyone. That was welcome news for me, because unlike Melanie Griffith in *Working Girl*, I never thought I had the body for sin. But my new job in the Big Apple helped me discover that scoring sex in the city is surprisingly easy.

One of the few benefits of being a celebrity publicist was that I got invited to every party in town. Event planners and promoters hoped to get in my good graces so that I would encourage my famous clients to attend their soirees. My celebrities on their red carpet meant mentions in gossip columns and pictures of the events in magazines like *US Weekly*. I was in the door at parties others only read about in *PageSix*.

Angela enjoyed helping me sort through all of the invitations that flowed in on a daily basis. When I told her I was suspicious of the one for *Cosmopolitan* magazine's Bachelor of the Year party hosted by Carmen Electra at the Royalton hotel, she shook her head.

"You might change your tune if you read the issue," Angela said.

She went to her room and produced the latest *Cosmo*. Flipping through the pages, I salivated over the men in various stages of undress—the photo portfolios in the magazine were like soft-core porn. One more button undone at the waist and we would have been ogling *Playgirl*. The Bachelor of the Year contest was like a male Miss America pageant—guy next-door types sent in photos and tried to write clever answers about why they should be the next chosen one. A boy from each state was nominated a finalist, and one crowned a winner.

"Look at their abs and tans. They're not all straight," I said.

"Only one way to find out," Angela replied.

The next evening, my black town car paused outside the Royalton Hotel. The boutique hideaway once seemed so mythic to me. Over a year after my first encounter, it now appeared worn like an aging pop star struggling to stay in the limelight. The doormen were cute, but not as imposingly handsome as I remembered. They yanked open the kingdom's gates that seemed just a little smaller than last time. Inside, a screaming coterie of lustful women had turned up to ogle two-dozen "straight" male specimens on display.

As one of the few men in the room not posed near a gigantic photo of my naked torso blown-up from the pages of the magazine, I stood out like a sore thumb. I grabbed champagne from a passing tray, and squeezed through a gaggle of women, finding myself at the edge of the party staring at a muscle-bound good 'ole boy. The dark-haired hunk caught me staring and winked. He spoke with a thick, sexy twang.

"Hey there, I'm Mister Mississippi. Who are you?"

"Texas? I mean I'm *from* Texas. Not *Mister* Texas. I'm just a guest here. Not one of the finalists."

"Well this here is my friend, Mr. Iowa."

He motioned to a blond farmer Adonis, who shook my hand a little too hard and put his arm around my shoulder.

"We saw you come in and we said maybe there's a guy who can show us around New York."

"Oh, sure, I'd love to."

I grabbed another champagne from another passing tray. The Southern charmer moved even closer to me.

"Maybe you want to see the room we're sharing. It's crazy. The bathroom is all glass. Have ya'll ever seen anything like that?"

"Not in a while."

I smiled, and gulped all remaining bubbly.

After my romp in the hay with the barely legal boys of *Cosmo*, I moved to the opposite end of the age spectrum and developed a thing for older men. I thought perhaps I needed someone more mature, a little more stable, someone who had real boyfriend potential. So I started looking for opportunities everywhere and found unrequited love when I accompanied actress Teri Hatcher to the first VH-1 *Divas Live*.

My boss BusyB assigned me the task of escorting Teri to the usual trifecta of morning show appearances: *Good Morning America*, *Regis & Kathie Lee* and a taping of *The Rosie O'Donnell Show*. Teri was between gigs, having ended her run on *Lois & Clark,* and was in town promoting a line of greeting cards with a breast cancer and Mother's Day tie-in. She had just become a mom herself and was traveling with her newborn. Most importantly to me, Teri was introducing Gloria Estefan on the debut of VH-1's *Divas Live*. I had always loved Miami Sound Machine.

After our morning show appearances, I stopped by Teri's hotel to escort her to afternoon rehearsal for the concert. The line-up of limos outside the Four Seasons New York was impressive even for the city's understated out-of-town celebrity hideaway. Running late, and blinded by the glistening spring sun, I jumped inside the nearest black stretch chariot, and tumbled unexpectedly into the lap of a sexy tanned gentleman in the back seat. I've always had a thing for Latinos and, with my developing appreciation of older men, this distinguished fellow took my breath away—handsome, dashing, available? I gazed at him dreamily with my head near his crotch.

"Excuse me, I believe you're in the wrong limo," he said.

"Oh, my goodness. I'm so sorry. I was just going to Divas Live with my client. Where is she? I'm so sorry. Are you going to the concert? Can we give you a ride?"

He just stared at me blankly. I thought he must be a Telemundo soap opera star.

Knock! Knock! Knock!

Through the darkened windows, I could see Teri tapping and shouting furiously at me.

"Wrong one, dummy. Our car is back here," she yelled.

Flush with embarrassment and a trace of lust, I grabbed my bag and papers, apologized and stumbled back out into the blazing sun. The Latino lothario smiled past me as I stood outside holding the car door. I watched silently as an equally glamorous Latina whizzed by and took my place at his side. Gloria Estefan bounced into the limo and rolled her eyes at me—another queen come to worship (at) her heels. I shouted as she shut the limo door and locked it behind her.

"I loved *Coming out of the Dark!*"

"Well, well, well. You just made a pass at Gloria's husband Emilio. Nice work," Teri teased.

"I think I'm in love," I panted like a cupid-struck teenage girl.

We ducked into our much smaller car a few places down the road and headed to rehearsal where the VH-1 *Divas Live* directing team walked Teri through her role at the famed Beacon Theater. Her job was to come on stage and introduce Gloria, the second musical number, with about three scripted lines, ending with, "Ladies and gentlemen, Gloria Estefan!" Seemingly simple, yet surprisingly grueling for Teri. She shielded her eyes from the spotlight, asking advice from anyone who would listen.

"Excuse me, excuse me. Does anyone know how to say Gloria's last name?" Teri asked.

An assemblage of VH-1 writers, stagehands, sound guys, gaffers, and flunkies gathered round.

"Can someone tell me how to do the accent? Is it ES-te-fan or es-TE-fan?" Teri continued.

Anyone standing nearby with a collectible *Divas All-Access Pass* felt obliged to give a conflicting reply, which confused Teri even more. I bounded onto the stage from the wings intending to rescue Teri from the accent vigilantes. That's when I noticed Gloria and the love of my life Emilio sitting in the auditorium watching the whole thing.

"I'm just going to ask them," I said, pointing into the audience.

"No! You can't talk to Gloria!" a VH-1 staff member insisted.

Her red color-coded badge gave her an extra level of authority over the other flunkies.

"You're kidding, right?"

I laughed and walk towards the steps into the audience.

"Do not walk off this stage. They are off-limits. No one is to talk to them!" the head flunky shouted.

"Look, there's no way Gloria and Emilio couldn't have heard all the nonsense on stage. I've already made a fool out of myself with Emilio once today, I've got nothing to lose."

Silence on stage as I descended the stairs and made my way to the middle of the Beacon Theater where the famous duo were seated. They were surrounded by a sea of celebrity cardboard cutouts posed in seats, used as stand-ins during rehearsals so cameramen know where to train their close-ups during filming of a live show. I passed by a stiff Sarah Jessica Parker and took a hard left at a listing Patricia Arquette. Emilio looked up from his reading as I made my way down the aisle and seemed panicked at the thought of what this crazy train might do.

"Hi there. You guys remember me from the car thing before?" I asked.

They shifted anxiously in their seats.

"Well, I'm back! Just hoping you could clear something up. The thing is, well, I'm Teri's publicist, and she doesn't want to mispronounce your name."

I sat down next to Emilio, my knees just brushing up against his, and he shifted his legs away from me slightly. I looked into his eyes and lost my train of thought for a second.

"So, anyway, sorry. I was wondering if you might give me some coaching? I mean give Teri some coaching. About your name. Do you prefer ES-te-fan or es-TE-fan?"

Emilio's tensed up broad shoulders relaxed, relieved that I wasn't as insane as I appeared. My heart melted. Gloria looked around at me.

"I'm just so honored that Teri is here to introduce me. I don't care how she says my name, sweetie."

Gloria said "sweetie" not in my too-familiar-Southern way, nor in the Yankee-slightly-judgmental way, but in a Latina-Pop-Star-Survived-Major-Trauma-Non-Diva kind of way.

"Wow, that's so generous of you. But really, I want to get this right. I mean, Teri wants to get it right."

"In that case, we prefer es-TE-fan," said Emilio.

His rhythmic sexy voice sent chills down my spine. I could hardly speak as I backed down the aisle and retreated toward the stage in a cloud of admiration for them both. I turned around, performed a little bow of thanks and could have sworn Emilio winked at me.

My crush on Gloria's husband paved the way for me to actually date an older man who was a tax attorney and turned out to have quite an unusual fetish.

Attorney was nearly 20 years older than me, and we met cute at Barney's in Chelsea where I liked to go score free samples of Kiehl's. He asked me for advice about a moisturizer, mistaking me for someone who worked the counter. I noticed his sweet face and expensive eyeglasses, casual preppy look, slight stutter, and an unassuming charm—think wit of Michael Caine with the delivery of Michael Palin. He took me to dinner at a little Italian joint across from his nearby apartment.

"I used to come here all the time with my partner. So it's a big deal for me to be here with you."

That made me a little nervous. I didn't really want to get into a discussion about his ex.

"So, you haven't been back since?" I asked.

"No, I pretty much come here alone four times a week."

That explained why the maitre d' greeted him by name and quickly escorted him to a table near the back.

"I always have the same table and order the same pasta dish."

I thought that sounded a little obsessive, but was willing to go with it—we all have our New York City coping mechanisms.

"How long has it been since you broke up?"

Was I dealing with rebound sex or serious dating potential?

"We didn't break up. He died about six years ago. From AIDS. We had been together ten years. You're the first person I've been out with since he passed."

I was completely unprepared for that guilt trip. Now, even if I didn't like Attorney, I was thrust into the role of dating rehabilitator—helping him get back in the saddle. I was worried that anything I might do would upset his recovery process.

"Why don't we order some wine? I need a drink."

After dinner we crossed the road and entered what looked like the Madison Avenue Ralph Lauren store, only it was Attorney's Chelsea studio apartment. He told me that he had hired then up-and-coming designer Robert Verdi to recreate the style of Polo inside his loft. No detail had been overlooked—the rich paint colors, plaid wallpaper, drapery fabrics, wood paneling—all had been copied meticulously from the bastion of preppy chic. It made my *Alphabet City* set look like it was decorated from the gutter.

He put on some Yanni tunes, and I tried to think of something to say about the stuffed heads of deer, buffalo, antelope and other exotic hunted prey covering the walls.

"All the animals sure are interesting. Where did they come from?"

"My personal collection of taxidermy. You should see the stuff that's still in storage."

I settled on the leather couch and looked up at the custom built cherry wood bookshelves. There was a stuffed screeching cat posed on a wood branch staring down at me. Remembering my run-in with Whoopi's cat, I thought it best to keep my distance. Attorney saw me looking at the preserved feline as he sat next to me.

"My cat just died so I put him up there."

"Oh my goodness."

I shifted nervously. Who has their pet stuffed? Screeching, no less. Maybe Attorney was a little more sinister than I imagined.

"Oh, no, no, no, no. My cat is in the antique urn up there. Next to the bobcat. The stuffed one was a present from my partner," he laughed.

As I looked closer around the room, there were framed photos of his beloved everywhere. Attorney edged closer to me on the sofa.

"I haven't had sex since he died. But I'd like to try tonight."

At that point, it would have just been plain mean to make a run for it. So we climbed into his enormous four-poster bed, stripped down, and he practically exploded—he hadn't done it with someone for years. But because he had back problems, he could only do it one-way. Literally. Which meant that night, and over the six months we dated and had sex, I was staring into the eyes of that screeching bobcat.

It sounds creepy, but Attorney was a really nice guy. I'd never been with a grown up that treated me so well. He took me to expensive dinners and paid for everything. Every time I stared into the eyes of the screaming feline and told myself I needed to break up with the Taxidermy Tax Attorney, he'd give me some expensive gift like a fancy suit or a watch and I just stayed.

One fateful night at the theater changed all that. He bought me tickets to see Liam Neeson on Broadway as Oscar Wilde—a present to compensate for his having to work late one night. The play opens with a guy performing oral sex on a chambermaid. The entire audience was shocked. I was riveted. Attorney was asleep—snoring so loudly that people were staring. At intermission, like a true-blooded theater snob, I insisted he leave.

The next day, he sent me a Palm Pilot as an apology, and then called wanting me to come over that night. When that image of the bobcat entered my head, I knew I couldn't do it anymore and told him it was over.

Even though I knew I was doing the right thing, I was depressed. It was easy getting lulled into false satisfaction believing that the comfort of expensive things can stand in for the excitement of love. Finding true bliss was turning out to be much harder than expected. The rest of my sitcom life was going well. Being a celebrity publicist provided opportunities for guest stars, even if it wasn't the most fulfilling job I had ever had. I just wished my dating story lines were meatier and more flexible.

But I had little time to worry about my love life because soon enough Tyra reared her gorgeous head. And this time there would be more trouble than I ever bargained for.

Next on *Alphabet City*:

Things go terribly wrong with Tyra in Turkey. "I trust you to fix this!"

Episode 7

Turkey Trouble

Jon Paul gets roughed up in gay Constantinople. Filmed on-location in Istanbul. Guest star: Tyra Banks.

A few months after Tyra's book tour concluded, my boss BusyB called with the news that I was going back out on the road with her—this time to Turkey. She was launching a new product line for Swatch called "Skin," and supposedly both the affordable timepiece and the international supermodel were huge in the Euro-Asian country. The best part was that I would arrive in Istanbul a few days earlier than Tyra, allowing me to explore on my own.

I shared the good news with Angela over a salad at the hole-in-the-wall Café 7A around the corner from our apartment.

"Turkey? That's far away. My passport is all ready in case I need to come get you out of prison or something," she said.

"Prison? What do you think I'm going to do there exactly?"

"I don't know, but I've read about Turkey. You never know."

I dabbed a side of carrot-ginger dressing onto my dry salad—I was trying to lose weight quickly in case I encountered some cute men on the journey. Angela continued, sounding like she was Sally Field in a *Lifetime* movie-of-the-week.

"Trust me, if there's anyone who knows how to marshal the full resources of the US Embassy to get you out of jail, it's me."

"I'll be with Tyra Banks for God's sake. What? You think I'm going to be arrested the minute I step off the plane?"

"I'm just saying be careful, and carry a condom."

In truth, I was looking forward to an exotic adventure and maybe some overseas sex. In the few trips abroad by myself, I had come to love the search for a little no-strings-attached vacation action. So, I loaded up on guide books, conducted mounds of online research, and discovered that despite cultural and religious persecution from a Muslim-tradition, Istanbul did have a small but teeming underground gay life—all centered around an unmarked disco, down the street from a park somewhere. A little mystery added to the sexiness. I packed a few Trojans along with my nothing-bad-will-happen-Mary-Richards attitude and set off in search of gay Constantinople.

From the moment my Swatch-provided guide picked me up at the airport, Istanbul smelled sexually exotic to me—an intoxicating blend of cumin and cardamom mixed with hard-earned sweat. While I lived in the city that didn't sleep, this ancient metropolis straddling Europe and Asia was spinning even more furiously. I remarked to my escort about the number of people rushing about, glued to their mobile phones, going, going, texting, and going.

"Turks work three times as hard to keep up with rest of Europe. Every minute Turkish lira worth less. What can you do?" he replied.

The guide cranked our car into high gear making a beeline for the Blue Mosque. Only 24 hours before a rendezvous with Tyra, so I needed to pack in all the sightseeing possible before her plane touched down.

That night, I struck out on my own and wandered around the edge of a large, dark park in search of Istanbul's gay underground. A shadowy figure appeared. I flinched, putting a hand on the wallet in my back pocket.

"You like dance?" he asked.

"No thanks."

I shook my head and couldn't remember a single Turkish phrase I had studied on the plane. I was an easy target, wandering around after midnight, lost with a map in my hand, trying to make sense of the directions I had downloaded off a gay travel web site. What was I thinking? I would never walk around the streets of New York telegraphing to the world I was a tourist. But one overnight flight later and all my defensive barriers collapsed. The figure stepped into the light of a street lamp and I sighed with relief and lust. He was an impossibly good-looking, blonde hair, blue-eyed Turk—think body of Brad Pitt with the eyes of Orlando Bloom.

"Is fine. Yes, yes. I take you to disco. This what you want, yes?"

He stuck his hand in the waistband of his tight-fitting jeans just above his crotch. I nodded, smiling. He grinned knowingly.

"No dance now. Now café."

In a crowded and brightly lit spot just off Taksim square, we sat drinking bitter Turkish coffee. The caffeine jolted my nerves.

"What-is-your-name?" I asked slowly, emphasizing every word.

"Name Aslan."

"Aslan. That's unusual."

It was silly to have mistrusted a handsome guy like Aslan. I was sure he was just being friendly.

"My name is Jon Paul."

"Like Bible?"

"Just like Bible."

I smiled nervously, wondering if I should tone down a Christian name in an overwhelmingly Muslim country.

"What-do-you-do?"

He just shook his head, flashed a grin and jumped up.

"We dance!"

Aslan lead me down some dark alleys and I glanced around nervously, calming when I saw his little butt shimmy in his tight jeans. He was cute, but not quite my type, really. I dreamed of coupling with a tall, dark, wavy haired Turk. He reached for my hand. Well, on second thought, maybe tonight Aslan could be my type. Yesterday I was lead through the filthy streets of *Alphabet City* tethered to a curly haired dog; now I was being lead through the medieval streets of Istanbul by a curly-haired lothario.

A pair of eyes peeked at us suspiciously through the slat of a steel door. One look at Aslan and the dance floor was ours. Inside, everything melted away to the sounds of throbbing techno and the sight of hundreds of exotic homos dancing under the glitter ball. I spun around, marveling at my good luck and adventurous spirit, as Aslan thrust his pelvis up against me and slapped a rough kiss on my mouth. I gently pushed him away. He motioned the international sign for cocktail.

"Drink?"

I nodded and he disappeared, and I began my disco lap around the multi-level club. The music was loud. Lights were flashing. The boys were staring. I was busy ogling locals who were busy ogling the tourist who had found his way. In this culture, I was the other. My head was spinning like it had earlier at the Blue Mosque, where I removed my shoes and stepped into a world of worship, and chanting, and religious fervor that filled my head with chaotic melodies. My mind raced to comprehend a place unlike any I had experienced.

My loins sexed up on a hunt for a Turk who would show this interloper the passion of his exotic world, I trained my arrow on the most deliciously striking man I had seen all evening. He was tall, slim, dark, with a wavy mane of black hair—think legs of Hugh Jackman with the curls of Antonio Banderas. He caught me staring and waved me over.

"You not from here, I am guessing."

He leaned in and I could feel his breath on my neck.

"Passing through. For work," I shouted over the music.

"What you do?" he asked.

"I'm here with Tyra Banks. You know her?"

"I love Swatch! I die to have Skin!"

He held up his wrist with no less than four Swatches on it.

"I'd die to get under your skin!" I teased.

He stared blankly. Either he couldn't hear or couldn't understand my attempt at flirting.

"My name Hakan. You dance!"

He grabbed me by the hand and led me to the dance floor. Every time Hakan brushed against me it was like an electric shock, sending an explosion through my body. He smiled and felt my growing crotch. He moved behind me and held me in his arms, swaying to the music. I felt sexy, and lucky, and safe and closed my eyes. Hakan stopped moving. I opened my eyes and there was Aslan. Not pleased.

"Oh hi, Aslan. This is Hakan."

I tried diffusing the situation with my Southern manners. Aslan scowled and wedged himself between my newfound love and me. He aggressively pushed the larger Hakan who rushed off the dance floor. I tried to go after him, but Aslan grabbed me and forced me up against him.

"Look, Aslan, I'm not that interested," I pleaded.

He shook his head and acted like he didn't understand me. He shoved the cocktail he was holding to my lips.

"Drink!" he commanded.

He forced me to take a swig. I wrenched away and ran to the bathroom.

Oh boy, this was getting messy. My head was spinning. I wasn't thinking clearly. Did I drink that much? As I turned the corner to the bathroom, there was Hakan.

"If you come with Aslan, must leave with Aslan. Bad things happen to you. To us."

I shook my head confused, bracing myself against the wall and watched Hakan disappear down the dark hallway. Aslan appeared and forced me to take several sips of another drink and then rushed me outside into a waiting taxi. My legs and brain started to feel heavy, clouded. We pulled up at my hotel, and Aslan escorted me through the lobby to my room. I tried not to make eye contact with the concerned desk clerk. They know me here. Know what I'm doing. Act like everything is okay and just keep going. This is almost over.

Once inside, Aslan stripped down and forced me to hold his flaccid dick.

"You make hard. You suck."

I shook my head, barely able to stand up. He forced me down on the bed and straddled me.

"No, get off me. Leave!"

He tried to hold down my arms, but I used my upper body strength and rolled him off the bed.

"Now get out of here!"

"Must pay. Give money!"

Just wanting it to be over, I pulled out all the Turkish lira in my wallet and threw it at him. I had no idea how much it was. He shook me.

"You rich American. Where is other money?"

He threw me back to the bed and began ransacking the room.

The smartest thing I had done was lock the money in the safe. My mother taught me that on our first trip abroad. Aslan rifled through the closet as I whimpered. Not able to move, I didn't know what else to do. I picked up the phone and dialed the operator.

"Send security, please."

Aslan tensed up. I held the phone in my hand like a weapon as he turned and gathered his clothes and the wad of cash I had given him. He moved close to me, but I just sat on the bed, my legs like rocks. Suspended in shock. He reared back and punched me in the stomach. I doubled over in pain, desperately trying to breath. The door slammed. I sat on the edge of the bed rocking back and forth, wondering how I let this adventure go so terribly wrong.

Slowly, that night, the embarrassment turned to deep shame. How could I have been so naïve? How had I let my lust cloud my judgment and spin so far out of control? Breathing heavily, I rocked myself on the bed and cried. At some point, I passed out.

***

The ringing hotel room phone wakened me from the depths of shame, signaling my car was downstairs to take me to the airport. It was already time to fetch my client. How would I keep all this from Tyra?

Still sluggish from what I assumed was a drug slipped into my drink, I rushed through the lobby the best I could. The night clerk was just ending his duty and smiled. I looked away nervously. The Swatch-guide looked me up and down and winked.

"You enjoy too much Turkish Delight last night?"

"In a manner of speaking," I managed.

With my attention focused on pursuing manly desserts, I had assumed everything was lined-up for Tyra's arrival. I reasoned that since I had gotten the hang of a U.S media tour, Europe wasn't going to be any different. Meet Tyra at the airport. Get her to rehearsal. Make a few appearances. Say "no" to a lot of people. Boom we're done.

"Don't worry about a thing. The airport has all been taken care of. Private VIP treatment for Ms. Banks!" the guide confidently proclaimed.

I should have checked all the details, but I was too busy picking up tricks in the park.

At the airport, the VIP team whisked me to the jet way where Tyra was disembarking. We would escort her through a special immigration and customs area, and she'd be on her way. I was on edge, everything made me nervous. Everywhere I looked I imagined a swarthy Turkish fellow trying to steal something from me. Even the airport signs were a jumbled mess of Turkish hieroglyphics to me. That way to the toilet or duty-free?

I stood on the jet way sweating as her overnight flight pulled up to the gate. The plane door opened. Tyra stepped off in her traveling outfit—track pants, hair pulled back, no make-up, glasses—looking like her "before" picture. I smiled and inched forward—and out of no where, dozens of paparazzi photographers came running down the corridor, descending on us, flashes going off, screaming in Turkish.

"What's going on?" Tyra yelled.

"I'm sorry. I'm sorry. I screwed up."

We dodged a torrent of flashbulbs.

What the fuck?! How did these jokers get past security? Where is our security? Fuck. Fuck. Fuck. We were deer caught in headlights. Tyra covered her head with a sweatshirt. We pushed past the photographers. They chased us as we ran through the airport. Was this the Turkish VIP treatment? Our Swatch guide grabbed us and rushed us to one side.

"Miss Tyra with me in car to the hotel. You stay and collect bags and Miss Tyra's passport."

"I'm not leaving my passport," Tyra said.

"No other option. Miss Tyra go with me this way now."

He motioned towards a passageway. Tyra shrugged, and before she ducked into a back door, she looked at me with a steely stare.

"I trust you to fix this."

Problem was, I didn't trust myself. Hours earlier, my confidence had been punched out of me.

A few minutes later, I stood staring at the baggage carousel as it spun around and around endlessly with no luggage in sight. The arrival hall was the size of Grand Central Station and filled with chaos. Shouting, stampeding, grabbing, eating, spitting. Now snapping. The paparazzi menacingly surrounded me, shooting me gathering Tyra's trunks that finally arrived. A guy arrived with Tyra's passport and hustled me to a waiting car that sped back to the buttoned up Swissotel. We passed the blackened Bosphorus strait on the way and I considered jumping out to avoid the dressing down from Tyra. While stuck in traffic, the driver unwrapped a box of candy and turned to me and winked.

"Turkish Delight?"

Not now, I thought.

Outside Tyra's room, I nervously tapped on her door. In her robe, Tyra peeked out.

"Hi! I just ordered lunch, and I want to hear all about your time in Istanbul and what you've been doing since book tour!"

She gave me a big, tender, meaningful hug. I leaned into her, exhaled all my tension and broke into sobs. She walked me to the couch.

"I hope you're not crying about that airport mess. Girl, next time you just need to carry a big wad of cash and pay everyone off!"

"Now you tell me. I needed that advice last night."

Over lunch, I launched into the whole sordid story of the previous evening with Aslan and my lost love Hakan. Tyra soaked up every detail like she as my best girlfriend, never scolding me, and again demonstrated her talk show advice skills.

"Well, put the past behind you. Focus on your potential love! Hakan sounds hot. Maybe we'll run into him. Never know, stranger things have happened."

She embraced me tenderly, and then clapped her hands excitedly.

"I want to buy a rug. Did you buy a rug? When can I buy a rug?"

"I'm not sure we have time. Our schedule is pretty packed, and you're due at rehearsal."

The main event of the Tyra Turkish Swatch Skin Extravaganza was a modern interpretive dance show in the ballroom of the Swissotel attended by the crème de la crème of Turkish society—including the Prime Minister. Tyra's job was to come out in a skin-tight leotard and prance around the fog-blanketed stage touching curled up dancers who were also dressed in skin-tight leotards. Tyra's "touch" was supposed to bring to life the dancers.

Instead, it brought on the giggles in Tyra and me. She eventually sent me away from rehearsal so she could get through it. The show was hokier than a Busby Berkley musical, but Tyra was a consummate professional and not only delivered her touches flawlessly, she gamely stayed and chatted with all the dignitaries in the room even though schmoozing was not part of her contract.

The next morning, the paparazzi followed us all over town—from mall appearance to mall appearance. The combination of two Turkish loves—Swatch and Tyra—had sent the town into overload. As we pulled away from the hotel, our guide turned to us laughing and handed over one of the daily tabloids with my picture next to the baggage carousel.

"You are famous, Mr. Jon Paul."

"You look terrible. That lighting is awful. What does the headline say?" Tyra asked.

The guide knitted his brow and pursed his lips, struggling for the right words.

"Translate directly it say Tyra Boy Toy. But much funnier in Turkish!"

Tyra and I laughed so hard we cried.

"I just hope your Hakan doesn't see this," Tyra whispered.

Turkish mall appearances were as predictable as their American counterparts with the same amount of weirdos proposing to Tyra. With fans lined up at the Swatch store in a mall to get their watchcase signed, Tyra passed me another box of Turkish Delight given to her by a stranger.

"I don't understand why you won't take me rug shopping," she complained.

"We can't just stop in any old rug store. There's an entire army of paparazzi trailing us if you haven't noticed. Rug shopping is not like looking for shoes. You have to put some thought into it."

I took my own decision to buy a rug very seriously. On my junior publicist salary, I made next to no money and had scraped together all the cash I had, and only then ended up with a little wool rug that cost about $300—an utter fortune for me.

"Next, please. Sir, Tyra is not signing calendars today, only watches," I announced, as if that made any sense in English or Turkish.

"How big is yours?" Tyra asked suggestively.

"I bought a small rug. They wrapped it tightly in brown paper for me to carry back on the plane."

"Well, I need one the size of my living room!"

Tyra signed her name with a big heart and passed it back to the lady who had purchased all seven varieties of Skin watches.

"Aren't you going to Africa right after this for a photo shoot? Good luck schlepping around that big of a rug," I replied.

After our last Swatch appearance, Tyra spied a rug store nearby and bamboozled me into letting her go inside. Any rug buying experience in Turkey is a theatrical production—they lay out many carpets in an effort to gauge your taste in colors and tolerance for price. But because it was Tyra, the shopkeepers put on an extravaganza, dragging out hundreds of the largest carpets I had ever seen—bigger than the entire *Alphabet City* set. I kept suggesting smaller rugs, reminding Tyra she needed to carry it with her, and the store kept rolling out larger ones—to Tyra's nodding approval. After much hemming and hawing, she settled on one that I believe cost my entire year's salary.

"Don't you think that one's gorgeous?" Tyra asked.

"It's gigantic," I said.

"Would you do me a little favor?"

"No way. Not a chance. I know where this is going."

"Might you carry that little rug back to New York for me? Please? I'll be your best friend for life," she pleaded.

"I'll think about it."

What a push over. I had caved. My job was to be a master manipulator—pulling the puppet strings of the media. But a supermodel had out maneuvered me. I didn't want to disappoint Tyra; after all, girlfriend had said all the right things about my Turkish love delight gone wrong. I ordered an extra mini-van just to get Tyra's chosen rug back to our hotel.

After a full day of paparazzi avoidance, Swatch launching, and rug shopping, we pulled up at the hotel exhausted. Tyra and I tumbled into the lobby and a tall fellow rose from the couches, clutching a bouquet, displaying four Swatches on his wrist. He began walking towards us with a determined stride and a big grin like he was crazy in love. Our security detail blocked his path, but I smiled and shooed them away.

"Tyra, I'd like you to meet Hakan."

His long arms enveloped me in a bear hug.

"These for you, Tyra," Hakan said.

He handed her the flowers. Tyra patted me on the back.

"Well, well, well. You got it going on, Mister JP. I want to hear all about it later."

Hakan and I rushed to my room where his presence turned the scene of a crime into one of passion. He explained in his halted English that he had waited all day long. He remembered I was with Tyra and had read in the tabloids where she was staying. He only knew my first name, so the hotel would not allow him to call my room or leave me a message—rightfully suspicious after my last visitor. So Hakan had waited patiently all day long in the hope of seeing me again.

We made electrifying love—the anticipation of it overwhelming both of us at times. He then escorted me to an elaborate dinner in a romantic restaurant where the twinkling lights reflecting in the Bosphorus sparkled in his eyes. I could hardly eat because I wanted to stare at him and run my hands through his hair. We relied on smiles and furtive touches because our ability to communicate through language was limited. Back at my hotel room, crammed into one of the two tiny twin beds in the room, we stayed awake and held each other all night, not wanting to acknowledge what we both knew—that this was it, really, we would never see each other again. We didn't know much about each other, but we knew enough to understand we lived in worlds separated by seas of difference.

The next morning, I crossed an ocean making my way home, but never forgot his tenderness, his sweetness and dogged determination to find me. When I arrived back in New York, Angela helped me drag into our apartment my traveling companion—Tyra's enormous carpet.

"How did you afford such a big rug?" she asked.

"Please, this is Tyra's. Thank God customs took my corporate Amex, or you would have had to come get me out of debtor's prison."

"How much did you have to pay?"

"Just shy of six thousand dollars."

I handed over the receipt and one of the eleven boxes of Turkish Delight I had picked up on the trip. Before I went to bed that first night back, I rolled out my little rug that looked like a fabric swatch compared to Tyra's behemoth. Winnie sniffed it and then promptly peed on it. It was good to be home.

A month later, Tyra called me in the middle of the night asking me to deliver her rug to The Regency Hotel where she was staying. Her magic carpet had cluttered the *Alphabet City* set for weeks now, and I was happy to clear it out. Tyra and I had a good ride together, but as it turned out, we would never see each other again. While being Tyra's Boy Toy certainly had its advantages, I was starting to tire of all the hand holding and babysitting it took to be a celebrity publicist. Did the glamorous travel, funny stories and celebrity encounters compensate for my lack enthusiasm for the job? Nothing would test my resolve more than my next trip to the *Rosie O'Donnell Show*.

Next on Alphabet City:

Trouble explodes when Jon Paul disappoints Vanessa Williams. "Your job is to make her look the best she can possibly be."

Episode 8

As Bees in Honey Drown

Jon Paul rises to the top but then nearly loses it all over Take Your Daughter to Work Day. Guest stars: Vanessa Williams, Rosie O'Donnell, Derek Jeter.

In the basement of 30 Rock, I paced nervously, five minutes early to greet the limo with my client that was now 15 minutes late. Today was a big day for me—I had been elevated to the top of the celebrity publicist pecking order by the sheer fact that I was accompanying the main guest for a taping of the *Rosie O'Donnell Show*. BusyB explained the details in one of *Alphabet City's* now-routine celebrity-laden plot set-up calls.

"Rosie is celebrating Take Your Daughter to Work Day. Vanessa is the first guest."

"The lead guest? Wow, that's big for her."

"And for you. I trust you to get this right. Do whatever it takes."

I had worked with Vanessa Williams a couple of times prior—she was one of the few celebrities that I was nervous about being around. I was worried that my gay-dolization of her over the years would impact my ability to calmly perform the duties of junior publicist in chief. I worshipped her despite—and probably because of—her career highs and much-publicized lows. At the time, Vanessa was in one of those lulls—other than a couple of TV movies, she hadn't worked in awhile. So getting to be the lead guest and sing with Rosie was an important moment. Since I was in charge of handling this very special performance, a lot was at stake for both Vanessa and myself.

Her *Rosie*-provided limo screeched to a halt in front of me. I gently opened the door and out flowed a volcanic eruption of tension. Vanessa's ten-year old daughter Melanie was crying, as was her eight-year old daughter Jillian, as was her five-year old son Devin, as was the twenty-something nanny Carol. Vanessa pointed at me.

"What's your name again? Never mind. Find Melanie's picture she's been working on for Rosie. She left it at home. Get in the car and head back to Connecticut."

"But I've never been to your house and wouldn't know where to look. How about Carol here head back instead?"

"All right, but then you have to take care of the kids. I need some quiet time to get ready."

Before I knew what was happening, Vanessa hopped onto the elevator and Carol climbed back in the limo. Vanessa's little munchkins, still whimpering, were now under my reluctant protective custody.

Talk show tapings are a race against the clock, and like Olympic athletes, the backstage players have their pre-event rituals. The minutes tick away as the celebrities tease their hair, show producers confirm guest anecdotes, and audience members warm up their cued applause and canned guffaws. A well-oiled machine like *Rosie* typically hummed along four days a week with little overt sense of panic or confusion. So when the elevator doors opened up into the backstage hallways that *Rosie* shared with *Saturday Night Live*, I wasn't sure what to make of the chaos in the corridors.

On first glance, I spied ballerinas spinning, magicians tricking and zookeepers feeding. We certainly weren't in Kansas anymore. I clutched the kids close to me and ventured into the hallway. One of the producers shouted at me as he whizzed by. It was my favorite talent booker Tommy—think southern charm of Matthew McConaughey with the beguiling smile of Robert Downey, Jr.

"We're doing two shows. In addition to Daughter Day, we're taping the 12 Days of Christmas special! We need you on set pronto to go over blocking."

"Any thoughts on what I can do with Vanessa's kids?"

"Sorry, we're jam packed today. I'd help you out if I could, but we don't even have a spare dressing room."

Tommy disappeared into the maze, and I shuffled my huddled masses past a colorized portrait of Gilda Radner and into Vanessa's dressing room. Her face was lit up glaringly in the klieg lights of the mirror, exposing every flaw that her make-up team was working furiously to hide.

"Where have you been? Any update on Melanie's picture?" she asked.

Just the mention of the lost treasure sent Melanie into hysterics, compounded by Jillian's tears, and Devin's wailing.

"Now kids, mommy needs to get ready for work. This man is going to take care of you, alright?"

Irritated that Vanessa still didn't call me by name, I patted the kids on the back and motioned for them to follow me back out into the fray. I wasn't at all sure where I was leading my little charges. As we left, Vanessa called out to me.

"Oh, and I need honey. For my tea. Make sure to come back with some honey!"

Back in the hallway, Tommy raced by my weary pint-sized relay team and me.

"We need you on set, now. Rosie wants to be at the final walk through, so we need your undivided attention. Lose the kids, please."

"Isn't this supposed to be take your daughter to work day?"

Tommy shook his head and shuffled off. Moving to the top of the celebrity publicist heap meant piling on a load of new headaches. Was there a Tylenol specially formulated for fallout from famous foibles? I was starting to resent the addition of "baby-sitting" to my list of job responsibilities. Out of nowhere, a baseball whizzed by my head, inches from breaking my nose.

"Oops, sorry about that! We were just warming up."

A tall fellow in a pin-stripe uniform waved, a leather glove covering one hand. I assumed the renegade baseball mob was part of the 12 Days of Christmas Extravaganza.

"Who are you supposed to be anyway?"

"10 Lords-a-Leaping," he replied.

On cue one of his teammates tossed a ball that he leapt in the air and caught. Little Devin tugged on my arm in excitement, and I looked down to catch him grinning from ear to ear. It was the first smile I'd seen on him all morning, and I had an idea. I looked up at the imposing athletic figure.

"Tell you what. How about I ignore the head injury you almost caused back there, and you give my little pal Devin here some pointers?"

The player ambled over, took off his glove and reached out to shake Devin's hand.

"Anything for our young fans. Hey there, I'm Derek Jeter."

Devin grabbed the baseball legend's hand and never looked back at me. I glanced at my watch—we were getting dangerously close to show time, and I still had two pre-teens under my command and was needed on the set.

Quickly, I entreated the 7 Swans-A-Swimming née New York Ballet to run through a set of pliés with Jillian, and grabbed Melanie's hand, racing onto the talk show set, where Tommy was going over last minute blocking with Rosie.

"Vanessa's daughter comes out, you chat about what it's like to go to work with a famous mom, and she hands you her picture."

"Do we know what the picture looks like so I have something clever to say?" Rosie asked.

"That's the problem. There may not be a picture. The girl left it at home," Tommy explained.

On cue, Melanie started crying and Rosie looked out into the empty audience seats to find the source of the whimpering. I waved from the aisles, rushed Melanie down the stairs, calling out to Rosie.

"Hi Rosie! Because of you, I wanted to be a VJ on VH1!"

"And who are you now?"

I could tell by the look on her face she was worried security had let some crazed fan slip in before show time.

"Oh, I'm Vanessa's publicist. This is her daughter, Melanie."

I fretted about how all of this was about to go down. I had heard that Rosie was famously temperamental in that Barbra Streisand perfectionist kind of way. I figured if anyone was getting blamed for the missing picture fiasco it was going to be the junior publicist in charge, certainly not the star. Rosie tilted her head and bent down to the little girl's level.

"Well, hello there. Now, why all the tears?"

Melanie was shell-shocked, so I stepped in, remembering something I had read about—the special day care Rosie had set up for her own children just steps from the studio. For Rosie, every day was Take Your Kids to Work Day.

"In all the excitement and confusion of the morning, seems like we left behind the special picture Melanie has been working on. We've sent the nanny back for it, but in the meantime, do you think it might be possible for Melanie to start on a new drawing? Maybe your own kids could help her out? I know that's asking for a lot."

I hoped that Rosie would understand the situation as a concerned working mother, and as a competitive talk-show host—she needed to keep her lead guest calm and on track just moments before airtime. I looked at her pleadingly. Rosie smiled at Melanie.

"You know what, I think my son Parker would be happy to share his crayons. Why don't you and I go back and ask him now?"

"Okay, but it won't be as good as the one I've been working on for weeks," Melanie uttered through stifled tears. Rosie took her hand.

"Don't worry about that. Whatever you do will be just fine by me, honey."

Honey? Oh my God. In my rush to find adequate and instantaneous childcare in Rockefeller Center, I had completely forgotten about the honey. I ran out of the studio.

As I sprinted down the hall, I jumped over a ground ball from Devin, avoided a high kick from Jillian and ducked into the infamous Green Room. Catching a much needed breath, and break, I tugged off my black v-neck sweater. I had planned on spending a lot of time basking in the glow of my top client's aura in this holding room—a glorified publicist purgatory. Instead, I worried that yellow sweat stains were seeping through my starched white shirt.

Had it all come down to this for me? A manic search for childcare and honey? I scanned the buffet desperately—the spread in the green room had reached legendary proportions in publicist circles. There were the H&H bagels with seven kinds of specialty cream cheese, and the expertly sliced exotic fruit, and of course three varieties of fresh squeezed juices, not to mention all the shade-grown organic coffee you could drink. Sweat was dripping from my brow, my face flush with excitement and dread. Where was the honey? Please let there be honey. Vanessa needed honey! Thank God, there were packets of bee's nectar just behind the sugar substitute and soymilk. I grabbed a handful of the sweet and sticky stuff, and took a deep breath on the way back to my client's dressing room.

This job was crazy. Was I wasting my time? My talents? On the one hand, I was proud of what I had accomplished so far—I had run a talk show obstacle course in record time—we were just thirty-minutes from show time. But on the other hand, I had my doubts about a job that required everything from gossip column denials for Liza to carpet storage for Tyra. I clutched the honey packets in my hand, thinking I didn't really have any other employment prospects. And besides, this job had its moments. Like spending time with Vanessa. This time, she would appreciate my efforts. This time, she would thank me by name.

I eased back into her dressing room, and gently laid down the honey packets at her altar, trying not to interrupt the hair and make-up team. As I turned to leave, I smiled to myself thinking maybe my calm nature and quick wit might just make me a successful celebrity publicist. Vanessa's melodic voice interrupted my personal reverie.

"When I asked for honey, I meant fresh honey. Not these packages."

As I turned around and met her pleading eyes, I was deflated, realizing there was one more ingredient necessary to bake a perfect celebrity publicist cake—desire. I might be even natured and resourceful, but the soufflé falls flat without desire. I no longer wanted to be a glorified Mr. Fix It. In my heart, I didn't care about the honey or the gossip columns or if Teri pronounced Gloria's name right. What had started as a nagging doubt after Turkey with Tyra turned into a full-fledged case of celebrity publicist blues during Vanessa's honey requirements. All I wanted was Vanessa to say thank-you for all I had done with her children, but instead she just wanted more from me. I didn't have any more to give.

"Hey, you know what? Best of luck today. I'm out of here."

I waved, turned and marched out the door. On my way down the hall, I leisurely passed the 12 Days of Publicists huddled in the green room, and waved good-bye to the flacks—this one had flown the coop. There were audible gasps of astonishment as I waited for the elevator. At the base of 30 Rock, I cell-phoned in my resignation.

"Can't say I'm particularly surprised. When your heart's not in something, you end up not doing a particularly good job," BusyB said.

"What do you mean? I think I did a pretty crafty job today, thank you very much."

"Crafty, perhaps, but not quality. The honey seems unimportant to you, but to her it means the world. Your job is to help her be the best she can possibly be. That means you have to not only know what's important to her, you have to anticipate it."

"How am I supposed to anticipate her needs if she can't even remember my name?"

"You're her junior publicist, not her best friend."

He had a point—that did sound a little whiney and needy. I watched the smiling tourists spill out of a nearby deli, coffee and muffins in hand to fortify their tummies after a long morning of shouting outside the *Today Show* windows.

"Look, I get it. You've done good work for me. But not everyone is cut out for this job. You're smart and the firm doesn't want to lose you. We'll find you something else to do. But there's a condition. I need you to see Vanessa through to the end of the show. Make it right."

Could I do that? Could I swallow my Texas pride and smoke a peace pipe with Vanessa? As I considered how I could possibly "make it right," a black limousine was just pulling up and I could see the nanny Carol waiving something at me from inside. I looked at my watch. Out of the deli marched three middle-aged women with matching red jackets and a crumpled poster-board proclaiming "Missoula Loves Matt." Each one was stirring cups of hot tea. I knew what to do.

"Listen boss, gotta go! Only thirteen minutes to air!"

A few minutes later, the elevator doors parted on the studio floor. In one hand I held tight to my newly acquired brown paper package and in the other I clutched a mess of construction paper and glitter. I sprinted past 9 Ladies Dancing née Rockettes and 12 Drummers Drumming née the cast of *Stomp*. Just past the perpetually laughing Gilda Radner, I tumbled into Vanessa's dressing room. She was cradling a cup of tea, shaking her head at the sight of me. I smiled as I handed over my peace offerings.

"Sorry about that. Here's Melanie's picture. And some fresh honey from the deli downstairs. Oh, and I took the liberty of picking up a real lemon as well. I noticed only fake stuff in the Green Room and thought you'd prefer the real thing."

She coveted the items as if I just delivered the gifts of the magi.

"Thanks, Jon Paul. I owe you one."

I smiled for the first time that day, knowing that I owed Vanessa a debt of gratitude. Wanting fresh honey wasn't too much to ask. It was my own attitude that needed an adjustment. I understood now that to be a great celebrity publicist you have to crave the diva details. You have to relish all the babysitting and the handholding. You have to love your mid-level place in the culture of celebrity.

At most, I was amused by it. I stood by collecting celebrity stories like I was an innocent bystander. But if you just stand watching from the sidewalk, life in the city that never sleeps passes you by. Vanessa gave me a kick in the pants to step off the curb and jump in to life, with the confidence to find something better. And she knew my name all along.

Next on Alphabet City:

Jon Paul's new duties take him to a land that time forgot—the Deep South. "Do you have the AIDS?"

Episode 9

Finger Lickin' Good

Jon Paul's new clients prove to be a challenge. Guest star: Gordon Elliott.

Soon after a self-imposed end to my celebrity publicist career, the firm gave me a job in the "Consumer Products" division. I would be doing for liquor and fast food all the things I had done for celebrities—get them on talk shows and into the gossip columns to create "buzz" about the products. First up was a program for Johnnie Walker whiskey called 'ScotsFest—a month long celebration of Scotland including a film festival, book readings, gallery shows and whiskey tastings. The plan was explained to me by my new boss Slick—think hair of John Stamos with the body of Tom Cruise.

"The more people like Scotland, the more Scotch they drink! You'll be managing some special Scots we're bringing over to help promote the event."

"A man in a kilt? Sign me up!"

As part of my 'ScotsFest duties I was entrusted with an assortment of crazy characters and told to get them on TV. My dreams of cavorting with hunky men sporting sexy brogues were dashed when I met my merry band of mischief-makers. They included three overweight kilt-wearing bag pipers, a couple of burly fellows from Edinburgh throwing giant wooden telephone poles, and a Glasgow chef carrying the smelly sheep's innards known as haggis.

How was I supposed to get this rag-tag bunch on TV? A producer at the local Fox morning show I had met while a celebrity publicist helped me out—on a condition: I had to go on a date with him. I was delighted that my time with famous faces was helping me get a leg up in the cutthroat world of consumer products. Young and single, the idea of an exchange of possible sex for a possible story didn't strike me as inappropriate. And so a deal was struck.

The regular shtick on this particular morning show was that Australian-TV personality Gordon Elliott would descend on an unsuspecting New York City neighborhood every morning. Broadcasting live, he would knock on a random door, and if allowed entrance, take over the house and broadcast the morning ablutions of the occupants—all while cracking jokes. Lucky for me, my Scottish misfits were welcome to tag along—Gordon and the producers thought it sounded hilarious.

Having never actually watched the program, I couldn't imagine who would agree to have their sunrise routine beamed to millions of viewers in the tri-state area on a regular day, much less when there was a motley crew of Scottish misfits involved. And not surprisingly, the citizens of Queens didn't open their welcoming arms that morning to Gordon and my plaid happy tag-a-longs.

We were turned away from cottage after cottage—despite Gordon's begging and pleading in his obnoxiously booming and often times unintelligible Australian voice. With valuable airtime disappearing, Gordon sped down the street, rejection after rejection, trailed by the wailing bag pipers, giant poles, odiferous haggis, and a crew of publicists and producers spilling coffee and dropping donuts. But our luck turned at the ninth house we approached that morning. The lady of the house jumped in excitement as if we were delivering a check from Publisher's Clearing House.

"Oh my God! It's Gordon! Come on in!"

Gordon was relieved that this housewife savior let him inside her humble home hoping for her three minutes of Good Day Fox fame.

The housewife's delight quickly turned to terror—the bagpipes screeched, and her lawn was decimated by the telephone poles from my Scottish sportsmen demonstrating the ever-popular Caber Toss. After two hours of back and forth live nonsense between Queens and the station's midtown studio, we left the yard in tatters, and the house reeking of sheep's innards. I left behind several bottles of Johnnie Walker—the woman clearly needed a recovery drink before heading to work. I wasn't convinced this was selling more whiskey.

Soon after I waved good-bye to the last bag-piper, Slick gave me a new assignment for Tanqueray Gin—working on a program called the AIDS Rides. Tanqueray had a sophisticated strategy for targeting the upscale gay population—tastemakers as they called them—by sponsoring major multi-day AIDS charity bike rides across the country.

"You'll love it. It's for a great cause. Biking for miles. Camping for days," Slick said.

"I'm not really the camping type. At least not in the traditional sense of the word," I said.

"No, you don't camp. The bikers do. You follow along in a car. Meet the riders at pit stops, arrange some press interviews."

For each ride, I got to know the heart-warming stories that compelled thousands of men and women to train countless hours and ride hundred of miles to raise money for AIDS services. Our goal with the PR efforts was to use the inspirational riders to garner press coverage—mostly in small town newspapers—and if they mentioned Tanqueray in the interviews, terrific! Hearing their tales of loved ones—gay and straight—lost to the epidemic often put into perspective my complaining about the shitty rental car and uncomfortable bed in a backwater La Quinta. It didn't stop the whining, just put it into perspective.

After having gotten lost from San Francisco to Los Angeles, and run a biker off the road between Boston and New York, I packed my sleek new sandals recommended in a recent *Wallpaper** magazine and headed off to Raleigh, North Carolina for the last ride of the season. The Raleigh-Washington, DC bike route wound through historic civil war sites and sleepy southern towns—most of which had never seen the likes of thousands of hunky bike riders sporting helmets decorated with feathers, glitter, beads and condoms. In one particularly long lost North Carolina village, the editor of the local newspaper, an elderly gentleman, caught up with me at the pit stop in his town.

"Now what are ya'll doing this for?" he asked.

"It's a four-day ride to raise money and awareness for AIDS," I rattled off.

"What's this AIDS?"

Goodness, this really was backwater. It was 1998, after all, not the early days of the epidemic. I wrongly assumed most of the press would know the basic science of the disease. But I did the best I could at explaining the current theory of HIV transmission, and he took copious notes. He flipped back through his pages, re-reading and marking items.

"How did you first know about this disease thing?"

He was like an editor that time forgot. He glanced down suspiciously at my sandals and scribbled another note. I was more than a little scared—for my safety, for this town, and for my job—the background interview had gone horribly off-track.

"You know, it's really best if you talk to the rider that's from this town. He can really give you a better answer," I explained.

"Alrighty, then, but one more question. Do you have the AIDS?"

Before I could answer, one of my favorite riders, a gentleman who rode in full-on drag with wig and heels and running mascara—breezed by and tossed some condoms in the air.

"Make sure grandpa knows how to use these!" he shouted.

Weeks later, back in the safety of New York City, and still nursing a bad case of swollen feet, a crumpled brown envelope with hand-scrawled letters arrived at my desk. I ripped open the package. Inside was a clipping from the local North Carolina paper that had discovered AIDS that fateful day. There was a handwritten note from the editor.

Thanks for teaching an old dog a new trick.

I smiled. There was a post-script at the bottom.

Where'd you get those sandals? I'd like to get a pair for my grandson.

The story he had written was one of the best awareness raising pieces I had read. And I thought it might just be the kind of episode that would earn *Alphabet City* an Emmy.

Because things were going so well with me handling consumer products like whiskey and gin, word arrived from Los Angeles that I was moving on up—out of my basement apartment into a proper New York office. More importantly, I was authorized to hire an assistant. So I did what you do in Texas when finding help—put an ad in the local newspaper, in this case, *The New York Times*. Within two days, my desk was flooded with over 800 résumés in response to the ad. But one applicant's submission got my attention immediately—she had worked for Medusa, a close friend of my first New York boss Madame.

When I worked on Billionaire's account at Madame's shop, Medusa called no less than ten times a day. God forbid the phone ring more than twice when she called.

"A proper office never allows the caller to hear more than two rings! Now put me through," Medusa chastised.

The first few times I had the audacity to ask who was calling, and my head was delivered on a platter. On other occasions Medusa critiqued the hold music, as well as my general demeanor—Madame told me that Medusa was suspicious of my Southern accent; to her, it made me sound stupid. In Texas, we would call her a "character," a polite euphemism for "raging bitch."

If this applicant could survive working for Medusa, then she must be the right person for me. A week later at her initial interview, I met Susan—think eyebrows of Brooke Shields with the sass of Kathy Griffin. She was close to six feet tall, towering over me when she vigorously shook my hand, and had a slight accent like me—only hers was from North Fork, Long Island not Southfork Ranch. She was tan, with dewy skin and silky hair, and the posture of someone at 23 years-old still coming into her own. She shifted nervously in her seat, eyes darting, as she tried to diplomatically reply to my questions about what it was like to work for Medusa.

"You know, I feel like I learned a lot from such a demanding environment. It was good for me," she began.

I smiled, knowing she was sugar coating the truth, and I appreciated the effort. She continued unconvincingly.

"There's a reason why Medusa is so successful and respected, and I wanted to learn from that. Medusa's office is small so it's difficult when there are personality clashes," Susan confessed.

I couldn't imagine her blending in with Medusa's team of mannequin flacks. I decided to put Susan out of her misery.

"Nice work, but believe me, I'm no fan of Medusa," I said.

"Well in that case, do you want to hear the real dirt?"

Susan's field hockey-toned shoulders noticeably relaxed, and over the next hour, we dished like old friends about a shared enemy. She revealed how Medusa's famous client, a TV personality, scolded Medusa and her team with the same type of criticism I had endured every time Medusa called—from hold music to phone manners. Medusa was guilty of doing exactly what gave top flacks a bad name—passing down the horrible treatment they received at the hands of their difficult clients to anyone lower on the totem pole.

"So, when are you going to hire me?" Susan asked.

I was charmed by her directness. Maybe she was a little rough around the edges, but so was I at one time. I could work with that.

"When can you start?"

I gave her a hug, thinking this just might be the beginning of a beautiful friendship.

A few weeks later, we moved into the firm's new Flatiron District loft office in the back of an advertising agency. The desks were crumbling and the computers malfunctioning, and I was already in love with the quirky space and congratulating myself on hiring Susan. She was a jack-of-all-trades—maintenance man, IT support, and caretaker—always worried about our next meal. She shuffled through a handful of take-out menus secured from area joints.

"Would you like to order in for lunch? What about sushi?"

"I don't eat sushi in summer. The heat makes me nervous."

"Well you're going to have to get over that."

She dismissed my odd quirk out of hand. Minutes later, my office was filled with a monstrous amount of Spicy Tuna and California Rolls, and we got to work on a new assignment from Slick. Kentucky Fried Chicken was rebranding to K-F-C in order to appeal to a hipper, younger audience. They had purchased advertising in the upcoming Academy Awards broadcast, which meant they had all kinds of sponsorship rights and were looking to the agency to come up with a plan to maximize their exposure. As the firm's resident hip, young, New York media-savvy employees, the task fell to us. I was pretty excited.

"My mother's favorite food is Kentucky Fried Chicken—this is going to be a lot of fun," I said.

Susan looked dubious. But I wasn't lying. On her birthday, my mother insists on three pieces of white meat fried in the Colonel's secret blend of spices. I was pretty sure I had the background to make this program a success.

"What if we served KFC backstage in the Oscar greenroom?" I asked.

"Julia Roberts dressed in vintage Valentino? Chowing down on greasy chicken right before she goes on camera in front of a billion people? Sounds like a recipe for disaster," Susan replied.

Clearly Susan wasn't going to have a problem speaking up to her boss. I appreciated her level of honesty. I began smiling from a crazy idea.

"Okay. What if it was a KFC gown? Remember the costume designer who won an Oscar for *Priscilla, Queen of the Desert*? She wore that special dress made out of American Express Cards? Well, what if we did the same thing—make a glamorous dress out of KFC buckets and lids?"

Susan nodded in appreciation, and like a good partner she helped build out the concept. We decided to dress models in these KFC gowns and have them deliver food to all the insane fans that camp outside the Oscars for days. Our first crazy brainchild was a hit with

Slick, and we were given the green light to make the KFC glamour gowns a reality.

With just a few weeks until Oscar time, Susan and I sprung into action. I hunted down and convinced a costume designer to take us on—she had come highly recommended by some of New York's finest drag queens. Susan turned the new *Alphabet City* office set into a storeroom for KFC paraphernalia—everywhere you turned were hundreds of the Colonel's red and white lids, buckets, boxes, cups and wrappers. Slick called from LA to check our progress with the KFC client on the line.

"I feel like we need something big in New York to showcase these dresses. What about having them outside the *Today Show* window?" the client asked.

"Brilliant idea!" Slick shouted.

Horrible idea, I thought. Susan agreed rolling her eyes at me. Stunts outside the Window on the World are probably the most ineffective way of getting a brand attention—the time and effort expended to secure an ounce of coverage never justifies the investment. For some reason clients love the idea, but Slick wasn't offering any truthful counsel.

"JP, can you make that work?" Slick asked.

I frowned at the phone and shrugged.

"I suppose if we had the girls in dresses pass out fresh coffee and biscuits, the fans would probably be thankful enough to hold up a KFC sign for us," I offered unenthusiastically.

"I don't know. I'm worried that serving the biscuits away from the store will denigrate the quality of the experience," the client said.

Now, I've eaten in a lot of KFCs during my life—from Texas to Tennessee—and never once thought about the "quality of the dining experience." The client was drinking too much KFC Kool Aid. I sighed.

"Well, we will certainly do our best to maintain the high KFC serving standards, sir," I replied.

A few weeks later, my black town car pulled up in total darkness outside 30 Rockefeller Plaza and I wondered how many more times in my life would I be here. At this exact spot. Escorting a client to *Rosie*. Or the *Late Show*. Or, like this morning, to the *Today Show*. The car was filled with the smell of fresh brewed coffee and buttery biscuits. I glanced out at the frost bitten lunatics who showed up with their hand-painted signs at four in the morning, scoping out the best spots near the Window on the World. There's that guy Joe who's here every morning. Creepy. Who's that next to him? Oh no, there's a problem. A big problem. A giant Oreo cookie dancing around. I turned back nervously to Susan and my fellow passengers.

"Code red. An Oreo cookie beats Kentucky Fried Chicken girls any day!"

A freak late-Spring cold snap shocked New York City the morning of our *Today Show* stunt—it was about 20 degrees outside. The KFC Glam Dresses had been designed to be sexy and revealing, with hints of skin visible through the chain links holding together the chicken couture. But with temperatures below freezing, my out-of-work actor friends had to wear full-length red leotards underneath the bucket dress concoction along with red and white stocking caps to fight the cold. Instead of KFC cocktail girls, they looked more like southern fried Santa elves. And now America's favorite cookie was celebrating an anniversary outside the *Today Show* windows—we were in danger of being muscled out.

"Never underestimate the power of a good cup of joe at four in the morning," Susan said.

She gave the gals and me a pep talk in the back of the town car, and then led the charge into the crowd.

"Let's do this in shifts, and get some air time!"

While Al Roker went for the cookies, our KFC ladies were a hit with the frozen fans—we were seen maybe twice while the show was going to commercial. The clients were thrilled and we were thoroughly chilled. But I was warmed by the thought that an important new character had been added to the permanent cast of my Mary Tyler Moore sitcom life. If Angela was my Phyllis, then Susan was my Rhoda—a New York best friend with a sarcastic edge. A new wisecracking character was just what *Alphabet City* needed to perk up the set.

I hand-carried the-one-of a-kind dresses to Los Angeles for their next deployment in the much balmier weather of Southern California. For two days, the KFC Glamour Girls headed up a team delivering fried chicken, biscuits, cole slaw, mashed potatoes and sodas to the lunatics camping outside the Dorothy Chandler Pavilion. Cameramen and photographers couldn't get enough of our models ministering to the hungry fans like Florence KFC Nightingale.

Pictures and video footage of the fast food Oscar dresses ran around the globe—from *Access Hollywood* to *Zimbabwe Today*. The client's favorite coverage? Not *Entertainment Tonight*. Not *USA Today*. Not even *People* magazine. No, they loved the photo of the KFC Glam Girls in a round-up story about Oscar fashions in that bastion of quality journalism, the *National Enquirer*.

Arriving back in New York City, my town car picked me up at JFK and ferried me across the Williamsburg Bridge, back home to *Alphabet City*. The twinkling view of Manhattan from the freeway energized me, amazed me—I was thriving in that urban jungle. I had left behind celebrity foibles and eased into a series of storylines focused on my creativity and wit. But while I tackled the new challenges with gusto, I had a nagging feeling that chicken and liquor could not sustain my interest for much longer—I was hungering for more.

Next on Alphabet City:

Jon Paul almost fumbles the chance of a lifetime. "Fun? This job isn't fun, JP. This job is hard work."

Episode 10

Blonde Ambition

After a trip to the North Pole, Jon Paul finds out if blondes have more fun at publishing giant Condé Nast.

There was a lot of time to ponder my future while I was stuck in grim Edmonton, Canada. I was PR commander at base camp for a group recreating Admiral Perry's famous turn-of-the-century dog sledding dash to the North Pole. The whole thing was as crazy as it sounds, dreamed up by my new client Doug Hall, an invention guru going through a midlife crisis. He was doing the stunt for the challenge and for charity, and hired me to promote it because of my AIDS Ride background. What was supposed to be a two-day project had turned into a multi-week boondoggle, and I didn't have enough clothes with me to survive the freezing winter wonderland. Even when I tried to make the best of it, I wound up alone in a Canadian gay country and western bar where Anne Murray was stuck on the jukebox.

Enough was enough. I had endured celebrities, liquor, bikes and now sleighs. While I had done some good work for the firm, and been steadily promoted, my advancement had slowed and I was getting antsy. My heart wasn't in agency life anymore; it did nothing to stir my passions. Under the Northern Lights, I vowed that when I returned I would have a serious story conference with the writers of *Alphabet City*, e.g. a soul searching session to find a new job.

A few days later, back in my office in New York, Susan welcomed me home by pushing me quickly inside my office, closing the door and waving several messages in my face.

"Hey Santa. This lady's been calling for you non-stop. Says it's urgent. She's the head of PR for Condé Nast. She obviously wants to talk to you about a job. I hear they're looking for someone to work at *Condé Nast Traveler*."

"Condé Nast? You're kidding. This could be big," I marveled.

As a kid in Texas, I was mesmerized by the world of magazine publishing. My father subscribed to two of Condé Nast's flagship properties—*Vanity Fair*, which I read cover-to-cover, and *The New Yorker*, which I acted like I read cover-to-cover. Later, in my role as celebrity publicist and gossip column reader, I could hardly escape the exploits of the famous New York publishing giant. And now I might be given the chance to peek behind the curtain of the famous empire.

A few calls later, and I found myself exchanging pleasantries across the desk of the head of communications for the company, SpitFire—think intensity of Diane Sawyer with the mothering of Olympia Dukakis.

"Frankly, since you were from Texas, I was a little nervous about how you'd look and sound. We have an image to uphold at Condé Nast."

As exhausting as it was to hear Yankees comment on my accent, I appreciated that she didn't beat around the bush. So I toned down the Southern drawl, and turned up the charm.

"What a treat to finally meet such a legend as yourself," I said.

She uncoiled from her seat like a spring and raced to shut the door, grab a bottle of water from her mini-refrigerator, and jumped into the seat next to me. She was just over five feet tall, but cast a tall shadow in the publicity world, a force of nature in her own right.

"Don't say legend. That makes me feel old!"

She copiously studied my suit, one of only two I owned, given to me by the Taxidermy Tax Attorney.

"Kenneth Cole? Thought so. Was just at an event *GQ* did for Kenneth," SpitFire said.

"That sounds fun."

"Fun? This job isn't fun, JP. This job is hard work."

She began rattling off a less than compelling list of reasons to join the company, including long hours and demanding bosses, all the while putting her legs on and off the desk, taking on and off her five Hermès bracelets, and yelling back and forth to her assistant.

"Tell Graydon I will just have to call him back!"

My head spun as she recited her impressive resume—working with a groundbreaking female TV anchor, being the right hand of a legendary female editor—and now working at the behest of one of the most important men shaping popular culture, Condé Nast owner S.I. Newhouse. She busied herself adjusting her bracelets again.

"We're the best in the business. No one compares to Condé Nast. And we're a family here. I want people who want to be part of a family. JP, do you want to be part of my family?"

I must have missed the part where she asked me about my background or told me about what exactly the job entailed at *Condé Nast Traveler*. But who could turn down the offer to be part of her family?

"Sure, I guess."

"Great. Then we'll move you along on the interview process. The wheels turn slowly here. There are many other people you have to meet before we make the decision to adopt you, as it were."

She laughed at her little joke.

"Oh, okay. The thing is, I was hoping for something a little sooner. My friends are starting a dot-com. They want me to come work for them as soon as they get their venture capital."

Once word got out I was looking to leave the agency, my friends tried to snap me up quickly. I could hardly understand the online product they were developing, but it was at least a step out of the agency.

"Dot-com? You'd consider going to a dot-com over Condé Nast?"

SpitFire was astounded. She had never met anyone who wouldn't put everything on hold for a once in a lifetime opportunity to work at the penultimate of publishing.

"Well, call me when—and if—you get a firm offer."

Her last words sounded like the final brush off, and I heard the doors to the glamour world of publishing shut with a clank. I felt like I had just applied for finishing school but screwed up my final interview. I tried to soothe myself thinking that the dot-com boom signaled the death of "old media." But I couldn't shake the feeling that for the kid from Texas the storied halls of Condé Nast held some magic that I'd never get to see.

When I got home, my phone was ringing off the hook—not with job offers, but with reporters desperate for a quote about my father. His legal license had been suspended. And he was blaming me. The life I left behind in the Lone Star state was reeling its ugly head. Despite my best efforts, the chain connecting me to my old life in Texas still tugged at its prisoner.

This particular link was an ugly family matter that I had tried leaving behind. About two years into college, I got a call from my father announcing unexpectedly he wouldn't send me any more money—claiming times were tight with his second family. I was desperate, begged, and he agreed to take out a Parental Loan on my behalf—if I promised to pay it back. I paid on the loan for years, but tried to leave behind the debt—and the anger—when I moved to New York.

I ignored the calls from reporters, and sunk into a funk. What kind of father throws their child under the bus like that? It wasn't my fault he ignored me when I told him he needed to live up to his parental obligations and start paying the bill. And, according to an article in the *Dallas Morning News,* I wasn't the only one he ignored. Bill collectors had been calling him for months trying to work out a deal, but he wouldn't speak to them.

After all these years, I wanted my complicated relationship with my father to just go away. Moving to New York was supposed to free me from his jurisdiction. As much as I wanted to speak with the reporters and set the record straight, I knew better than to play his game. As a publicist, I learned that if you don't feed the media beast, it eventually will look for story food elsewhere.

I needed something drastic to shake me out of my doldrums and disappointments. Not only did I want to escape old family drama, but I also needed a life beyond promoting whiskey and fast food. The one bright spot on the horizon—a chance to jump to the glam world of luxury magazines—had been extinguished almost as soon as it had appeared. Evidently the kid from Texas didn't have the finesse and sophistication for the sorority of Tina Brown and Anna Wintour. I needed to jolt myself out of an impending depression. So I turned to a bottle for help.

The next day, my head was tingling in pain. I had convinced my hairdresser—and myself—that dying my hair blonde would solve all my problems. As the chemicals seeped through my hair and into my scalp, I hoped the bottle of peroxide would jump start my depressing life. But after my first weekend as a blonde, I wasn't convinced. And neither was Susan when I showed off my new locks.

"Very bored New York gay boy if you ask me."

"Yeah, I think it's actually been bad for my sex life. Scaring off men. But I have some good news. My dot-com friends got their funding."

"What are you going to do?"

"Give the agency two weeks notice. I'm out of here."

"No silly. About Condé Nast. Didn't SpitFire tell you to call her when you got a firm offer."

"Oh that. I think she was politely trying to get me out of her office."

"SpitFire doesn't sound like the kind of person to bullshit. You'll never know if you don't make the call."

As usual, Susan was right, and within minutes of my phoning, SpitFire cleared her schedule and laid out a fast-track interview-audition-adoption process with a promise that Condé Nast would make a decision in two days. She explained the obstacle course I was about to run.

"First, the tough as nails Publisher. Don't worry, no one gets along with publishers. And after her, the charming Editor. He'll love you," she said.

The next day, I brushed off my other Kenneth Cole suit and headed up Madison Avenue to the company's intrigue-filled offices. If all goes well, I might just need Mary's Evan Picone wardrobe after all.

These were the days before the striking headquarters in Times Square with the Frank Gehry-designed multi-million dollar cafeteria. The magazines were housed in a collection of stuffy old offices spread out amongst many buildings, and *Condé Nast Traveler* was in a stepchild spot a few blocks away from the venerated *Vogue* and *GQ*. The luxury travel magazine's offices were dumpy and filthy, bordering on hazardous. Not at all what I had dreamed.

After a brief wait, I was escorted into the offices of Publisher—think confident demeanor of Glenn Close with the no-nonsense attitude of Debra Winger. I had prepped for my interview with Publisher by reading *Citizen Kane*, an unauthorized biography of Condé Nast owner S.I. Newhouse and the machinations of the company that now arguably defined much of luxury in America. In the book, Publisher was depicted as overly competent, but jerked around by the company's male management—including once moving her to a different magazine while she was on maternity leave. There was a reason why the company had earned the nickname "Condé Nasty" for their habit of chewing people up and spitting them out. She was wearing an understated but elegant pantsuit, accented with tasteful silver jewelry, and got right to business as we sat at the conference table in her office.

"I need a PR person who can think of ways to add some glam and sizzle to the magazine. We need to infuse this magazine with the Condé Nast DNA, do you know what I'm going for?" she asked.

I was drawn to her confidence immediately. She quizzed me about my time with Tyra and Johnnie Walker, and shared with me her determination to turn the magazine into a successful, moneymaking property.

"Are you ready for hand-to-hand combat with the enemy?"

I looked lost.

"I'm talking about *Travel and Leisure*. They are the devil!"

She was aggressive and intense, but also smart and gutsy. She constantly surveyed my outfit—suit, shoes, glasses, the works, as if I was pledging her sorority, and she was the rush captain. She browsed my résumé with a furrowed brow, and looked up at me.

"You know what I dislike? When people put down names of references thinking I won't call. I see you've got Billionaire down on the list. What would he say if I called him right now? And I will call. He's a client of the magazine."

Without hesitating, I gave her Billionaire's private number that I still remember to this day.

"I spoke to him this morning in advance of our meeting. He said for me to tell you hello. That's his direct line by the way. Not too many people have that."

I relaxed. She broke into a grin.

"Impressive. You've made it through the tough part. Compared to me, Editor will be piece of cake."

Editor did not feature at all in the Newhouse biography, so I had less to go on. But from what I gathered, he'd had a long run at the magazine—coming up on his 10th year—the second or third longest reign next to Anna at *Vogue*. He had won many coveted Ellies, the Oscars of the magazine world, including a recent one for "Best Magazine." Insider friends at Condé described him as "the nicest man in magazine publishing"—incredibly talented, and most of all, generous and caring.

I sat on the couch outside his office waiting, and after thirty minutes, out popped Editor—think smooth grace of Cary Grant with the comforting smile of Robert Redford. A sophisticated and lovely addition to the *Alphabet City* cast, I thought. He breezed away.

An hour later, I was still waiting. Editor often passed by and glanced over his old man reading glasses at me, and then looked back at his assistant, who just shrugged. He was wearing an uninteresting pair of baggy gray slacks, a polo shirt a size too large, and tattered loafers. No one around here gave him any wardrobe counsel?

I reminded his assistant what I was there for, to which she just shrugged. After another hour, the assistant shrugged and told me to go in Editor's office.

Editor sat at a large round marble table in his office, studying some papers in his hand, not making any indication he was aware of my presence. I glanced back out at the assistant wondering what to do, and on cue, she shrugged. I stood. Editor read. Without looking up, he motioned in one sweeping gesture for me to sit in a chair at the Knights of the Roundtable opposite him. I sat. He read. I fidgeted. He read. Who told me this was going to be a piece of cake?

He gently put down the papers, moved the reading glasses to the tip of his nose, peered at me, clearly begrudging the distraction I had become.

"What in the world do I need with a PR person?"

The supposedly nicest-man-in-magazine-publishing had asked a rhetorical question after he kept me waiting for two hours. I sat silent.

"Let me be clear. Why, at this point in the life of a very successful magazine, would I need to involve myself with someone engaged in the practice of public relations?"

Now I was plain mad. I could care less about going to work for this boob.

"I'm not really interested in selling you on the idea of public relations. Congratulations on your ten-year anniversary, and awards. Maybe you don't need any help. But a word of advice, keep on the same path, and eventually your image will become tired and boring."

I grabbed my bag and stuffed a recent edition of the magazine inside. I smiled, pleased with myself. He snatched off his glasses and raised his voice ever so slightly.

"This magazine has never been one to rest on its laurels. We have a whole range of new ideas—including a celebrity-themed issue in September."

"That's great. But without someone telling the world, you'll be a magazine that no one buys."

I stood up to leave and offered to shake his hand.

"Sit back down. I'd like you to take a look out these windows."

Editor made a sweeping gesture to the Midtown skyline surrounding us outside. He spent the next hour and half giving me a lecture as if I was attending a graduate school seminar in magazine publishing. He was no piece of cake, but he might just be my Lou Grant.

The next day at my office, SpitFire phoned. I was pretty confident about the interviews so her screaming was unexpected.

"Is there something you want to tell me?"

"I thought it went pretty well. We all seemed to get along, eventually."

"What about your appearance?" she barked.

"I don't know what you're talking about."

My Kenneth Cole suit was much better tailored than anything the editorial staff was wearing.

"Your hair?" she yelled.

My blonde ambition tour had completely escaped my mind.

"You interview with me and have brown hair. Several days later you're blonde. You thought no one would notice?"

"Does it look that bad?"

"Publisher called and said, 'he's terrific, but that hair. I'm not sure that yellow hair is the Condé image.' What do you have to say for yourself?"

I stalled for time, not wanting to admit to the sad ploy I had hatched to boost the ratings for *Alphabet City*. But I was determined to not let the Condé glamour slip through my fingertips again. I nervously looked around my office for inspiration. Susan had put a picture of me with the team of Canadian sled dogs from the North Pole project on my desk with a note, "Iditarod here I come!" I began spinning an elaborate tale.

"This is going to sound crazy. But I made a bet with my team on the North Pole project that if we got a huge amount of media stories, that I would do something crazy like dye my hair."

There was silence. It seemed to be working, so I continued.

"I had no idea we would do it. But we did it. And so I did it!"

"I'll get back to you."

She hung up, and I was pretty sure the blonde rinse on my hair had washed away my chance to join the fraternity of cool kids in publishing. Friends told me not to worry—the world was changing—and magazines were gasping for air, when there was no stopping the online world. But this Dallas dreamer just couldn't resist the temptation of the high-stakes, glamour world of publishing. It seemed so New York—so what a Mary Tyler Moore wannabe would end up doing.

Dejected, I packed my bags for a last minute getaway to the Virgin Islands—a little sand and sun before I began my new life on the information superhighway. I resolved to dye my hair a normal color when I returned—this blonde might be ambitious, but it was delivering neither jobs nor dates.

A week later, I was escorted back into the inner sanctum of Condé Nast. Publisher gave me a huge welcoming hug.

"Dying your hair blonde—that clinched the job! Anyone who would do that for a big win needs to be on my team! I've been telling everyone that story. Unbelievable!"

Yikes, how would I ever get out of this one? I guess I would just go with it—people believe what they want to believe.

"Now, what are we going to do about this?"

She threw down a *New York Times* story about competition heating up in the travel magazine category. The column reasoned that Condé Nast was upping the ante by moving such a tough cookie like Publisher away from her previously successful assignment at a home decorating publication. A competitor's quote said, "She should go back to selling shower curtains." Publisher was fuming.

"Let's wrap up some shit in a shower curtain and send it over to him with a big bow! How about, that?"

Shit was right. What had I gotten myself into? I raced back to my new office and called Susan—the new *Alphabet City* setting was going to need some serious character reinforcements. I had a feeling this luxury flight was going to be much more turbulent than I expected.

Next on Alphabet City:

Surviving a meltdown by Boy George, Jon Paul decides to spit on Scarlett Johansen. "Oh my God, more of a diva than we anticipated!"

Episode 11

Bold Faced Names

Jon Paul lands in the gossip columns after tussling with a male model. Guest stars: Boy George, Mark Vanderloo.

Being a publicist for a luxury travel magazine turned out to require a completely different skill set than promoting whiskey and fried chicken. For one, I wasn't begging reporters and producers to include my clients in a story. Instead, they came to me for access to *Condé Nast Traveler's* stable of experts. I quickly learned that the recipe for success was two fold: one part celebrity publicist—a lot of saying "no;" and one part air traffic controller—a lot of coordinating multiple requests into a smooth landing. If *CNN* wanted to talk about the latest plane crash, I told them "no," making sure not to associate the brand with disasters. If *Access Hollywood* wanted to talk about celebs in St. Barth's, I told them "yes," making sure the magazine was the go-to authority on all things glam. And if *Good Morning America* wanted to talk last-minute bargains, I told them we'd do hot hotels for great value—*Condé Nast Traveler* was chic not cheap.

Between the time of my interview and my first day on the job, the magazine had moved to the 14th floor of the company's new flagship headquarters known as Four Times Square. If you believed the sensational New York media, the world held its collective breath during the entire building process. It seemed like gossip columns and architecture critics covered the installation of each windowpane and the tightening of every bolt. During construction a crane fell into a nearby SRO hotel fatally injuring an elderly lady inside, and from the front-page tabloid coverage you would have thought that billionaire owner Mr. Newhouse himself had ordered an execution-style killing.

I found everything about the headquarters intimidating—even riding the elevators. Ascending to the offices of *Condé Nast Traveler*, I passed a floor-by-floor display of the most important media titles in American culture—*Gourmet, GQ, Vanity Fair, Architectural Digest, The New Yorker* and *Vogue*. Forced into sharing a small space with the fashion bible's famous guru Anna Wintour completely unnerved me. She had a habit of standing in the front of the elevator, turning around, taking off the ubiquitous shades, and staring at what every single person was wearing. I worried what she thought of my Banana Republic prêt-a-porter ensemble.

Thankfully, I had a comrade-in-arms to help steel my courage against the judgmental eyes of Condé Nast colleagues. The smartest thing I'd done a few months after my arrival was convince SpitFire and Publisher that the task at hand was more challenging and complicated than initially presented. If I was to put this publication on the proverbial celebrity buzz map, I needed first-rate back up to juggle all the demands. In short order, I was given approval to make Susan my deputy.

Within a few days of Susan's arrival, we began a tradition of giving each other daily affirmations of our wardrobe choices. It was important to keep a stiff upper lip in a competitive culture obsessed with the latest handbag and must-have sunglasses.

"You look cute today," Susan said.

"Thanks, Anna gave me the once over on the way up. Is this sweater working hard enough?" I asked.

"Definitely. The purple goes nicely with your skin tone. Remember, Banana Republic is a big advertiser. Their money is as good as Gucci," Susan said.

The problem for my bank account was that I was starting to believe my money was better spent at Gucci than Banana Republic. Condé Nast exerted mind control over wardrobe choices—being around all that luxury fashion made you believe those items should be part of your closet. My baseline of normal shifted. Up until now, my *Alphabet City* wardrobe included an odd mix of funky East Village pieces with a dash of classic Armani Exchange. But I quickly fell into the habit of routinely buying $400 Prada's—convincing myself that a mark down from $600 made them an irresistible bargain. Why I was practically saving money by purchasing them!

One of the most buzzed about features of the Condé Nast building was the "employee cafeteria." It was like nothing I had ever experienced. The space's gleaming blue titanium walls with handcrafted cantilever glass panels and beech white floors would have made Superman feel right at home. But this Frank Gehry-designed architectural masterpiece—rumored to cost nearly $35 million to erect—was built not for the man of steel but for the super hero editors of Condé Nast. They needed somewhere special to dine in the still seedy area surrounding the new headquarters shorthanded in the press as 4X2. So the unassuming and media shy owner Mr. Newhouse built a design Mecca cum luxury food hall.

The first day the cafeteria opened for business, Susan and I rushed down to check it out.

"We didn't have a sushi bar in my high school lunch room. Should we try the stir-fry or wood oven pizzas?" I asked.

"Looks like the *Vogue* girls are going for salad. Typical," Susan said.

It was the like being back in high school. What should I wear? Where should I sit? Do you think he's cute? Everyone played out to type—if the hung over *GQ* boys were the school jocks, then the studious *New Yorker* nerds were the Honor Society, and the slightly snotty *Condé Nast Traveler*s were the French Club.

"How about we sit here?" I asked.

I motioned to a banquette near the cashless registers— corporate i.d. cards were scanned at checkout like a debit card. It wouldn't have surprised me if it were a scheme for the company to keep track of employee's daily caloric intake.

"That's where Mr. Newhouse sits, according to *PageSix*," Susan replied.

"Speaking of *PageSix*, we need to get to work on inviting celebrities to the party," I said.

Susan's mention of the legendary gossip column reminded me that one of our most important duties was inviting famous faces to attend whatever soiree of the moment the magazine was hosting. Our strategy was scanning the gossip columns for names of possible celebrity attendees—if they were in the paper it usually meant they were making the rounds of parties searching for publicity.

"What about Mary Louise Parker?" I asked.

"Love her. Seems like she's in between projects. How about Marcia Gay Harden? She's out and about."

"Hello? Oscar-winner and fellow Texan? Definitely. Hey, what do you think of Chloe Sevigny?"

"I'd spit on her," Susan said without hesitation.

"What? What do you mean you'd spit on her?"

I couldn't figure out what Susan meant. Since she was always teaching me new hip-hop language, I wondered if this was some kind of new code word?

"There's just something about her that creeps me out. If I saw her on the red carpet, I'd spit on her."

"Wow, spitting is kind of gross isn't it?"

"Absolutely, you have to be really committed to it."

We spent the next hour ignoring stares from fellow diners wanting our coveted booth, and discussing exactly the parameters of who'd you spit on and why. We determined that spitting isn't really a rational activity—it's some guttural response to an individual that you just can't quite name.

"I'd spit on Scarlett Johansen," I volunteered.

"Really? I think she's so pretty," Susan protested.

"I know. But there's just something about her I find slimy. Like you said, there's nothing rational about it."

And so, during that lunch, out of Susan's dislike for Chloe Sevigny, we created one of our all-time favorite games, "The Spit List." Some general rules were established. Your Spit List doesn't have to be long. But it can't be people like Bob in Accounting—it has to be some kind of public figure and preferably not a politician like George Bush—that's too obvious. People can move on and off your Spit List for no reason. Over time, the easiest way to get onto the Spit List was to misbehave at an event, which is what happened at the magazine's first big celebrity party when I nearly had a meltdown over Boy George and a male model.

My first stab at infusing *Condé Nast Traveler* with the celebrity buzz of sister title *Vanity Fair* was the creation of a raucous glam event celebrating the magazine's Hot List issue—the best new sexy hotels in the world. The challenge for our magazine was that while famous faces willingly attend *GQ* or *Vogue* parties because an appearance at a sponsored event might lead to a career-enhancing cover, there's no built-in celebrity draw for a travel publication.

From experience, I knew that celebrities loved freebies, and our currency happened to be travel. I reasoned celebrities would attend our event if we gave them free trips—but for budget reasons I needed to get those getaways donated by travel companies interested in gaining celebrity exposure to their properties. A publicity win-win for all involved: the magazine, celebrities and the hotels.

So I convinced Editor and Publisher to host the magazine's first glitzy party in honor of the Hot List. We would throw the event at a much buzzed about new venue, basically hire a sexy crowd of people, and desperately wrangle up some celebrities for the event with the promise of travel compensation. The days leading up to the magazine's first Hot List party were filled with anxiety. And I ran around like a PR shrink dispensing medicated answers.

"Will anyone attend? What am I wearing? What is Editor wearing?" Publisher asked.

"I've got Susan filling the room with a cool crowd. I've got the fashion department pulling in some terrific options for you. I'm going shopping at Bergdorf's with Editor. Don't worry, I won't let him wear those awful loafers."

The biggest concern was from Editor—he was incredibly nervous about the idea of gifting celebrities with thank-you vacations for gracing our red carpet.

"It shouldn't be too obvious. I don't want it to look like we are giving away vacations in exchange for their attendance," he told me.

"There's no chance of that," I lied.

Of course, pay for play was exactly what we were doing. But in the early days of compensating celebrities for appearances, everything was hush-hush and under the table. Given my boss' concerns, I concocted a Willy Wonka-inspired scheme for that first party where every attendee received a ticket to claim a gift bag at the end of the evening. Seven of those tickets matched up to bags with a thank-you trip to New Orleans, and we made sure to give those winning tickets to celebrities. The Golden Ticket we made sure to give to our biggest name and it matched up to a gift bag in which lurked an all-expense paid vacation to Mexico's luxury Las Ventanas al Paraiso.

The plot worked like a charm. The chance that any party attendee might win a magical gift bag enchanted the gossip columns, and they ran multiple columns about them. That translated into lots of people trying to crash the party. Exactly what we needed since RSVPs looked a tad bit low. Of course, I knew that not just anyone could get the golden gift bag—we needed to make sure it was our biggest celebrity, and just happen to have a photographer on hand to capture the Kodak moment for later distribution to the press.

That night at the newly opened Chambers Hotel in Midtown, the party seemed to being going off like a charm. There was a line outside waiting to get in. Paparazzi shouted vigorously and shot furiously. The Mistress of the Red Carpet, Susan, looked pleased at the semi-famous faces posing for pictures. But I was flummoxed.

"I don't recognize any of these people," I said.

"Some MTV VJs and a couple of aging boy band members so far. But I hear Miss Universe is on her way. She'll go to the opening of a paper bag. How's it going downstairs with Boy George?"

"Oh my god, more of a diva than we anticipated!"

The 80s singer was trying to make a comeback as a DJ, and we had flown him in from London hoping he would raise the profile of the party. We scored a media coup when *The New York Times* was interested in following him for one of their "Night Out" features in the Style Section. But Boy George was acting like a baby and throwing a temper tantrum. He wouldn't come out from behind the DJ booth to talk to the reporter and was refusing to listen to any more of my reasoning that this profile could help his career.

Drunk dancing near the DJ booth, the guy I was dating overheard the kafuffle, swigged another shot of tequila and jumped behind the turntables to save the day. He hugged and slobbered on Boy George proclaiming my genius until, for the safety of all involved, the Culture Club front man agreed to speak to the Gray Lady's culture reporter.

"Pretty much the biggest name we've got here is that male model Mark Vanderloo," Susan said.

"Really? A little sad that he's the best we can do. But we're running out of time. Let's do it," I replied.

It was time for Operation Gift Bag. We caught Mark as he was running out the door—and "surprise" he had the magic ticket. He shrugged, completely confused. I handed him the luxury gift bag. Mark smiled. Cameras snapped. Flashes popped. The gift bag giveaway was captured for posterity. Mark had no idea what hit him, nor that he would soon be on his way to a Mexican spa.

When we let the gossip columnists know about the winner, *PageSix* was particularly snarky and suspicious that a male model won the trip—models got to travel all the time they argued.

"It simply isn't fair," the columnist complained disingenuously.

As if "fairness" was core to *PagSix's* code of journalistic ethics. The columnist immediately called Mark's agent who began backpedaling, ultimately denying his client had won. *PageSix* called back asking if was I lying, which infuriated my Texas-sized sense of integrity. The fight was on.

"Mark won the trip. He had the winning ticket," I told them.

Well he did. No one had to know that I handed Mark the grand prize coupon on purpose. More back and forth. *PageSix* was incredulous that both sides stood their ground. I was stupefied by

Mark's rep—was he playing some sort of game or was he just plain stupid? Mark had nothing to lose by taking the trip. It's not like his vapid client had some kind of squeaky-clean reputation to uphold. *PageSix* badgered me some more. At that point I was exasperated, and lost my cool.

"If Mark doesn't want the trip, I'll give it to someone else."

And that was the quote *PageSix* had been looking for. In the column the next morning, instead of the usual generic listing of me as "magazine spokesperson," they attributed it to me and published my full name—in bold-faced type. There was no missing the man behind the scandal, me.

Publisher came rushing down the hall to my office door waving a copy of the *PageSix* gossip column that treated the Vanderloo Gift Bag Scandal like it was the second coming of Watergate.

"Have you seen this? Why didn't you tell me about this?" Publisher yelled at me.

Susan ducked her head to avoid the line of fire. I assumed I was about to lose my job over this infraction.

"Unbelievable! Home run! Exactly the kind of gossipy press this magazine needs!" Publisher exclaimed.

She gave me a big hug and a bottle of Veuve Clicquot she had hidden behind her back. I craved a big swallow of the champs to calm my nerves in the topsy-turvy world of Condé Nast; I never knew exactly how things like this would play out. I had seen others vilified for the similar feats. But for now, I was heralded as a star for getting the magazine some ink in the columns.

There's a saying in Manhattan that immigrants to the city become true New Yorkers after living in the Big Apple for a decade. But in the publishing world you've arrived when you become a bold-faced name in the most famous gossip column in America, *PageSix*. That night, as I rode the elevator back to the lobby, I stood a little taller—proud that I had survived, and truly arrived. And Mark Vanderloo became a permanent addition to my Spit List.

Next on Alphabet City:

Jon Paul's mother pays him an embarrassing visit. "Have I ever told you about how Paul just loved superheroes when he was little?"

Episode 12

Even Jesus Needed a Publicist

The holiday season brings a visitor from Texas. Guest star: Graham Norton.

After moving to Manhattan, I replaced Texas holidays with New York's own December traditions. In addition to the Rockefeller Center Christmas tree, Rockettes at Radio City, and window displays at Barney's, there were more personal *Alphabet City* rituals like the annual dinner with my born-again Christian Korean Dry Cleaners, Peter and Paige. Over the years, Angela and I had become such reliable profit generators that the husband and wife team invited us every year to a thank-you meal at Christmas time. At first, I tried to convince Angela to decline their offer—who wants to share a meal with a service-provider like their dry cleaners? Angela persuaded me otherwise.

"Turning them down seems dangerous. Keep your enemies close, and your dry cleaners happy," she said.

There was also our own holiday party on the set of *Alphabet City*. Instead of traditional invites, I sent out Press Alerts—an insider joke for people working in the entertainment industry—entreating people to come to a "cast party" on the set, and encouraging their "publicists" to submit names of clients who might want to be invited. In 2000, one name appeared on the list that made me extremely nervous—my Mother.

Over my life, we had a roller coaster of a relationship. She doted on me as a kid, and I thought of her as glamorous and confident—a society woman who raised and educated the kids while my father worked. Several times, she whisked me off to Europe where we waltzed in Vienna and enjoyed theater in London. But when she remarried, Mother retreated to her native East Texas—trading in her cosmopolitan life in Dallas for a life in the country.

At 15, I moved in with my Dad and was left wondering what happened to my doting mother, who only occasionally reappeared in my life. When I officially came out of the closet a few years later, Mother stopped speaking to me and did not attend my high school graduation. In college, Mother hosted my sister's wedding at her house but would not allow my partner and me to attend together. She told me that her husband couldn't tolerate our lifestyle. It was as if my mother and I were in an extended boxing match in which we would emotionally bruise each other, return to our corners, regroup and then call it a draw.

While it was tough going, our relationship began an upward swing about the time I decided to move to New York. Her second husband had died and she began opening up to me again, even loaning me money to help me get settled in the Big Apple. But this visit worried me. I had worked so hard to build a new life away from the trauma of the Lone Star state. Could I trust Mother to support my life in New York?

Things got off to a rough start on the very first call when she announced her visit. I explained that I would be sending a car and driver to pick her up on arrival at Newark. Her reaction was a mix of Southern shock and comic guilt—think singsong pitch of Rue McLanahan with the timing of Betty White.

"What kind of son doesn't meet his mother at the airport?" she asked.

"It's not like Texas, Mother. People just don't do that here."

"Well I'm not talking about 'people.' I'm talking about my son. I never complained about picking up your father no matter what time it was."

It was pointless to argue. Mother's own airport shuttle service was legendary. When I was six, my father arrived early one morning on a flight from Japan. The day before, Mother loaded me in the car at 4am to conduct a practice run. She was concerned that she might miss the highway's exit to Dallas' newish airport. Never mind that we had been there many times and that the freeway dead-ended at the terminal. Mother was a worrywart.

A few weeks later, I was standing at Newark's baggage claim to greet Mother. She yelled as soon as she spotted me.

"Paul, just look at you!"

"Thanks, Mother. But I go by Jon Paul, now."

"Oh Paul, quit trying to be so fancy."

Barely five feet tall, she looked me up and down, taking notice of the red strip peeking out from the heel of my expensive loafers.

"Would you look at your shoes! Do they light up or something?"

"No, Mother. They're Prada's."

"Well, they sure are some New York shoes!"

I was guessing that "New York" was a euphemism for "gay." This was going to be a long visit indeed. And I just got more flustered in the car on the way to the apartment, when Mother began questioning me.

"Tell me again what kind of a job you have," she said.

"I'm a publicist. We pretty much have something to do with anything you read in the newspaper."

"You work with Erma Brombeck? Her column keeps me in stitches!"

"No, Mother. I don't work with Erma. I actually think she passed away."

When I moved to New York, she offered to loan me her well-worn copy of the famous humor columnist's book *If Life is a Bowl of Cherries, What am I doing in the Pits?*

"Tell me you don't do the horoscopes. I've always hated those."

I paused for a moment thinking how I could possibly explain my job to my Baptist-raised-turned-later-in-life-Methodist mother. Then it hit me.

"Okay, think of it this way—even Jesus needed a publicist!"

Mother gasped, but I soldiered on.

"Think of me like Paul from the Bible. He wrote all those letters telling everyone about Jesus' life. I do the same thing writing press releases!"

"Don't be smart with me, young man."

Maybe I wasn't being entirely fair to my mother. She wasn't the only one who didn't understand what it means to be "in PR." At New York parties, get-to-know you questions begin with "how much do you pay for your apartment?" and end with "what do you do?" Whenever I answered public relations—rather than an easily understood field like advertising or banking—the inquisitor stared blankly and then nodded knowingly.

"Oh, you throw parties."

That reply I found exhausting, if not just a little true.

When Mother crossed the threshold of my apartment, her high-pitched twang sent Winnie into overdrive.

"Hi there Winnie! Come get a little treat from grandma!"

"Mother, please don't feed her."

"Paul, you just need to rest."

Mother had been telling me "to rest" my entire life. It was an all-purpose expression meant to make me relax on command. As an adult, I was constantly repeating the mantra to Winnie, who ignored it just like I did as a kid. Mother produced some dog treats from her purse and Winnie scampered off. I showed her around the apartment, and she nodded approvingly.

"Oh Paul, I'm just so relieved. It's not anything like I pictured."

"What's that supposed to mean?"

"That it's nice. I was so worried that it would be awful. I told myself to be ready to get a hotel room just in case."

That was a classic Mother comment. At first, it sounded like typical parental concern. But where was all this worry the past six years? I had been in this apartment since I moved to New York.

I needed reinforcements, so I made sure that Angela could join us for dinner at Pisces, a seafood restaurant around the corner that was one of the more respectable joints in the East Village. It was my go-to spot for out of town visitors, but Mother looked uncomfortable.

"Oh, I don't know. You just need to order for me. The menu seems so complicated," she said.

"Mother, it's just seafood. You're the one who taught me to love oysters."

"Paul, that was so long ago. I'm a simple country girl, now. Don't forget to order me a Tanqueray and tonic."

Angela stifled a laugh, and then summoned the waiter for some stiff cocktails all around. When the drinks arrived, Mom really let me have it.

"Angela, have I ever told you about how much Paul just loved superheroes when he was little?" she asked.

I groaned. Angela grinned and shook her head.

"Well, Paul loved playing Spiderman so much, that he wanted to have his own special costume. He couldn't be like all the other little boys. Oh no, he always took things to the extreme."

"Gee, I can't imagine that," Angela teased.

"So for his sixth birthday, I told him to make up a new superhero and I would sew him a costume. And you know what he came up with? The Ferret! Well I had never heard of such a thing!"

"Alright Mother, that's enough."

"No, I definitely need to hear the rest of this," Angela said.

"Paul had just been to the zoo and held a little ferret. So his mind was made up. I sewed him this little brown tunic with gold sash and a mask. And he loved it so much that wore it every single day for months. Every single day."

"What kind of superpowers did The Ferret have?" Angela asked.

"I think my specialty was finding lost neighborhood cats," I said.

"The worst part was he'd crawl along the back of the couch while I was reading. Scared me half to death!" Mother said.

"What happened to The Ferret?" Angela asked.

"Well, Paul was just so obsessed. That brown costume was the only thing he'd wear. I was so worried. So I took him to see our pediatrician, Dr. Moore. He just laughed and told me not to worry. That Paul would outgrow it. A few weeks later, Paul was running around the backyard chasing around after that cat Pfeffa, and the seams ripped right up the back. His little bottom was hanging out for all the world to see!"

"Lord, Mother. Don't tell anyone else here that story, okay?"

"Oh, I think it's cute. I, for one, feel so much safer knowing Alphabet City is protected by The Ferret," Angela laughed.

The next day, I used all my publicist skills to put together a jam-packed itinerary that would have made even Tyra proud. I figured the busier I kept my Mother, the less time she would have to embarrass me. We went skating in Central Park, shopping at Macy's and touring around Ellis Island. A three-hour Circle Line cruise that circumnavigated Manhattan featured a tour guide who pointed out all the architectural highlights. It was just the kind of thing my mother loved. I relaxed until we headed back into port at 42nd Street and the tour guide made one last comment.

"Folks, there's a new building on the skyline. That tower with the spire is known as Four Times Square, the headquarters of the magazine publisher Condé Nast. You've probably heard of many of their titles like *Vanity Fair* or *Vogue*."

My mother leapt to her feet in excitement. She waved her arms at the tour guide who was standing a dozen rows in front of us.

"My son works at that Condé Nast! At the travel magazine! He's in PR!"

I shrunk from embarrassment, while my mother encouraged me to stand and wave at the crowd. As we disembarked, she was insistent.

"I wish you had told me we were going to stop by your office," she said.

"What do you mean?"

"Well, I didn't see it on our schedule. But since it's so close, we might as well. If I'd known I would have put on a different outfit."

Again, there was no arguing with her. And there was no telling what the ladies of Condé Nast would make of her denim ensemble. But as we walked the halls of the luxury empire, Mother charmed my colleagues with her Southern accent. She loved hearing my behind-the-scenes tales of the company, especially the story about the fancy Italian-designed filing cabinets that only held European size paper. The problem was discovered only after we moved into the new building, and we couldn't put away any files for months until a solution was finally found. Mother got out her camera and took a picture of one of the cabinets.

"That just kills me! The girls back home won't even believe it when I tell them!"

After the office tour, on our way to the elevators, I had a panic attack when I saw my boss Publisher barreling down the hallway. I had hoped we wouldn't run into her. While I loved Publisher, she had a bit of a judgmental edge that comes from growing up in Connecticut and graduating from Harvard. I had no idea what she would make of Mother, but there was no escaping the chance encounter now.

"JP, I heard that your mother was here. I hope you were bringing her down to meet me!"

She looked my mother up and down, just like she had done me when I first interviewed. Before I could say anything, Mother stepped right up and shook Publisher's hand.

"Jon Paul has told me how much he enjoys working for you. And I'd like to tell you how much I love your magazine. Especially the ads. The car ads are my favorite."

Publisher smiled. Mother winked at me. It was the first time she had referred to me by my full name. And how did she know that there are no sweeter words to a Publisher than a compliment about the advertisements? On our way out, I questioned Mother where she came up with that line.

"Oh Paul. Give your mom some credit!"

The next day, we busied ourselves shopping for the *Alphabet City* holiday party. Mother insisted on making her "famous queso"—a dip concocted from a hunk of Velveeta cheese melted in a slow cooker with a can of Ro*Tel Diced Tomatoes and Green Chilies. Aghast at the lack of choice and small aisles in our grungy neighborhood grocer Key Foods, Mother pulled out her camera.

"The girls back home are not going to believe this either!"

I was a little worried how Mother would fit in with the quirky assortment of characters expected at the party. Because of the way I sent out the "invite" disguised as a press alert for an "Alphabet City Cast Party," there was invariably someone who showed up thinking they were coming to a soiree for an actual television program. This year, I listed the event as happening at a new "underground East Village club." But anyone who knew me well, and had been to the party over the years, recognized the address as my apartment.

With the queso all warmed up, and Mother and Winnie perched on the couch ready to accept visitors, I opened the door to a gullible TV-producer friend of mine who had taken the Press Alert seriously.

"Um, hi, so what is this place? It's so underground that it looks like a real apartment. I guess normal is the new cool," he said.

He was trying desperately to look hip and in the know and not a bit surprised by the glaringly bright kitchen lights and wafts of garlicky spaghetti sauce. He twitched nervously and motioned to his friends standing nearby.

"These are my friends Kathryn and Graham."

He had brought along the local TV entertainment reporter who thought she might score a scoop, and British chat-show host Graham Norton. Graham thought he was being escorted to the latest invite-only club—one that was on the cutting-edge of chic tucked away in a tenement building with no sign and no velvet rope. I smiled at my little ruse.

"Welcome to the set of *Alphabet City*, the sitcom of my life. It's a very special episode. My mother is visiting from Texas."

After the initial shock wore off, Graham grabbed three plastic cups filled with wine, a plate of meatballs, and some queso. He found a spot on the sofa next to Winnie and Mother. I ran the other way when I heard the beginning of their conversation.

"Graham, have I ever told you how much Paul just loved superheroes when he was little?"

The next morning, Mother was up at the crack of dawn, packed and ready for her flight that didn't leave until three o'clock in the afternoon. She looked shocked at my pajamas when I stumbled into the kitchen around lunch time, hung over and looking for coffee amidst the debris of the previous evening.

"Is that what you're wearing to take me to the airport?" she asked.

"Mother, I ordered a car for you. I'm sure you'll be fine."

"What if I don't understand what they're saying at check-in?"

"As far as I know, at American Airlines they speak English."

She rolled her eyes, and I poured a cup of coffee. Winnie joined us on the couch, curling up between Mother and me.

"Well, I enjoyed the visit. And loved meeting your friends. That Graham was a hoot. Why don't you date him?"

"I'll keep that in mind. You know, I'm glad you came."

"Your life is turning out so well, Paul. But you're never coming back, right?"

"What's that supposed to mean?"

"Just that you never really belonged in Texas. But here, you fit right in."

"Thanks, Mother. I'll take that as a compliment."

Then she reached in her purse and handed me a twenty-dollar bill.

"Some walking around money. Take care of yourself."

The apartment buzzer rang. Winnie barked. Mother's ride to the airport had arrived. She gave me a quick hug, and then Winnie and I packed her into the black town car. She asked me to reassure her that the Holland Tunnel was safe, and told me she would call me from the airport to let me know everything was okay. As the car pulled away, she waved.

Mother and I had a complicated relationship, but we had reached a level of détente on this trip. She was right—I fit in better in New York than Texas. And then I felt a little pang of guilt—maybe I should have escorted her to the airport.

Next on Alphabet City*:*

Jon Paul picks up some tricks of the travel trade. "Babylon makes dreams come true!"

Episode 13

Babylon

Jon Paul travels the world in style with his new family. Guest stars: Rupert Everett, Peta Wilson.

As SpitFire promised in my first interview, working at Condé Nast was like being adopted into a family. And this family's vacations were like nothing I had ever experienced. If the girls of *Vogue* lived in the fashion closet coveting Yves St. Laurent, the boys of *Traveler* lived out of their luggage in rooms at the Four Seasons.

It all began innocently enough just two months after I started at *Condé Nast Traveler* with a trip to the Caribbean—a family getaway with my newly adopted parents Publisher and Editor. As they explained to me, my job was to handle the press for a kids' essay contest sponsored by the magazine. Every year, the publication staged an elaborate awards ceremony at a different Caribbean capital and flew in the eleven year-old finalists representing each island nation. It sounded so relaxing and charming, and I looked forward to a little beach time on someone else's dime.

Like a typical teenager, I packed all the wrong clothes having assumed the Dominican Republic was casual and laid back. But under the roof of the sweltering Santo Domingo convention center, men formally dressed in suits and ties. I was also ill equipped to deal with the onslaught of press surrounding an accusation that our little winner from Haiti had cheated. The press rushed the podium demanding answers and I panicked.

"We're going to need to work on your preparation. You should have anticipated this," Publisher lectured.

As we traveled to 14 countries together, Publisher took advantage of every opportunity to teach me lessons in planning. On each trip, she insisted that I drag around multiple copies of the current issue.

"You never know when you'll need it as a calling card," she said.

Publisher demonstrated her theory in Cairo where we were attending an exclusive travel industry gathering. Typical of the insider-privilege our magazine connection afforded, we were scheduled for a sunrise private tour of The Pyramids before they opened to the masses. A motley crew of soldiers with guns protected the antiquities that morning and blocked our car from passing. Our driver-translator was meeting firm resistance from the rag-tag guards in tattered uniforms. But Publisher was nonplussed in the face of resistance.

"Did you tell them who we are? Give me a magazine! I'll take care of this," Publisher said.

She grabbed the latest issue from my hand, jumped out of the car and marched right up to a gentleman in fatigues sporting a burly mustache. I scrambled behind as she waived the magazine under the soldier's nose.

"We are V-I-P! Very important magazine!" she shouted.

The Colonel tightened his grip on the gun slung over his shoulder and shook his head. Publisher flipped through the first few pages and paused on the masthead, pointing at her name in large, bolded font.

"That's me. See? V-I-P! V-I-P! Do you understand? V-I-P!"

With one nod from the Colonel, the back-up soldiers quickly fell into line behind their boss, fingers on triggers. I probably would be hauled into the US Embassy to account for the diplomatic standoff we were causing. Panicked, I looked back at our driver for any signs of assistance. He was on his cell phone, motioning for us to retreat.

"Miss! Miss! At wrong entrance. So sorry. Must go now!"

I put a hand on Publisher's shoulder and she took a step back. The soldiers relaxed. I breathed a sigh of relief. Publisher stared at her nemesis and then stepped back up looking him right in the eyes. Everyone tensed.

"I'd like you to keep this. My gift to you," she said.

She handed him the magazine and gave a little pat on the arm. He smiled. As we sped off, the Colonel and his cohorts flipped through the glossy pages. Publisher turned to me.

"Having that magazine came in handy. One day that gentleman could be the Minister of Tourism, and he might just advertise," she said.

It was hard to argue with Publisher—under her firm command she had transformed the magazine into one of the most profitable stallions in the Condé Nast stable. For over a decade, she worked closely with my other work parent, Editor. They made quite a team with a mutual fondness hard to find in many other publishing pairs. They balanced each other nicely: Publisher was high-energy and emphasized preparation; Editor was low-key and encouraged exploration.

Editor reigned supreme over a publication that, like *Vogue*, was the Bible of its industry. Because of that power, he was often referred to as the "Anna Wintour of travel." But my work-dad was much more approachable than his famous fashion colleague. Together we visited 16 countries, and I discovered his basic travel organizational skills were surprisingly lacking—I can't even count the number of broken reading glasses, forgotten suit jackets, missing cuff links, and lost PDA's. He was a mess, but he was my lovable mess.

Editor earned my trust in Berlin, a city I found particularly unappealing in early spring—drab, drizzly, depressing. We found ourselves in Germany's quickly modernizing capital city for an enormous travel conference the size of seven football fields. By day, we ran a gauntlet of travel promo booths—dodging imposing costumed characters from Kazakhstan to make our meeting with Japan's very formal Minister of Tourism while struggling to be heard over Tahiti's karaoke machine blasting *Margaritaville*.

By night, I was itching to discover why German boys had a reputation for kinkiness and headed out to a hot bar I had read about online. The club was in a sketchy neighborhood that sounded like it belonged in *Alphabet City*—filled with artists, drug addicts, and underground nightspots.

The doorman at the unmarked venue had purple-spiky hair, a giant nose ring, and a thick accent.

"Would you like to check your coat?" he asked.

I was confused since I was not wearing any outer garments. It wasn't really cold enough to put up with a coat.

"Not mandatory, but most people check," he said.

He held up a garbage bag in one hand, and a magic marker in the other. I shook my head and stepped into the club.

Techno music throbbed as my eyes adjusted to the dark. Figures darted about, chatting in the corner, laughing, and dancing. Most guys had their shirts off. Normal New York gay disco scene, really. My eyes adjusted more, and upon closer inspection I realized these guys weren't wearing pants either. My goodness. In fact, they had no clothes on.

What a dope. I had misunderstood the doorman—he was asking me to check my *clothes*, not coat. My fellow patrons had deposited their attire in a trash bag and marked their shoulders with a number allowing them to run a bar tab—no clothes meant no pockets for money! How clever. In a tight t-shirt and jeans, I was completely overdressed.

I sidled up to the bar next to a hot guy—dark skin, curly hair, reminiscent of my Turkish delight. He had a very nice package—it was hanging out on display. I had a hard time keeping my eyes above the waist.

"Where are you from?" I asked.

"Cyprus. Here for the conference."

"Me too! What do you do?"

"I work for the Cyprus Tourist Board."

"What a coincidence—I'm meeting with them tomorrow."

"Really, what do you do?"

"I work for an American travel magazine."

We paused, took a sip of our Vodka tonics, and then turned back to each other as it hit us—we were meeting with each other tomorrow, only with our bosses in tow, and pants around our waist. Awkward. I jumped up, and shook his hand.

"So listen, I need to run. Getting up early. To meet with you!"

I stole one more glance at his crotch. It was tempting to stay.

The next morning, in a car on the way to the conference, I nervously paged through our schedule and rolled the window up and down. Editor sensed I was out of sorts.

"You seem agitated. Maybe you've had too much coffee," he said.

Would he think this situation was funny? We'd been traveling together for a couple of years now. He probably knew I went out exploring. But how deep do I go here? He's married, with kids, lives in Westchester. On the other hand, I heard stories that as a single guy he had a wild streak. I took a deep breath and came out about the no-pants bar. He paused, then smiled and laughed until he was blue in the face.

"You're kidding? That's genius! We're really meeting with this guy this morning?" he said.

"You're not freaked out I told you?"

He reached out and put a reassuring hand on my shoulder.

"Freaked out? Travel is about adventure. Collecting experiences. Young man, I hope more of those stories are in your future. And I hope you recognize the fellow with his pants on."

When not traveling with one of my work-parents, I was typically paired with my Condé-sibling Mark. As the magazine's fashion director, Mark was like a half-brother who had been shipped off to English boarding school and came back a flamboyant character from *Bewitched*—think smooth moves of Pierce Brosnan with acid tongue of Ricky Gervais. He eyed me suspiciously when I told him a Travel Channel show called *Destination Style* was following him to the Spanish Mediterranean city and my job was to make sure the show was up to "magazine standards."

"Goodness, do you have any idea what those standards might be?"

I blanched—his British accent laced words with a dose of condescension. He smiled.

"Not to worry! I'm just the man to show you. We'll have great fun! But first, let's take you shopping for *proper clothes*."

Traveling with Mark through nine countries producing as many television programs was like being in a make-over show hosted by a gay James Bond. In Madrid, we drank Absinthe and purchased Loewe leather jackets. In Jamaica, we rented jet skis at Golden Eye and selected tie-dyed sarongs with actress Peta Wilson. In Paris, we partied at the couture shows with Rupert Everett and bought Louis Vuitton sandals. In Sydney, we raced on Harley's to Bondi wearing our leather jackets, sarongs, and sandals, flirting with the possibility of some action Down Under.

Mark always reminded me that we were representatives of the most influential travel magazine in the world.

"In every hotel, all eyes are on you, watching," he told me.

I learned that lesson first-hand on my virgin trip to the Far East. The magazine dispatched me to Asia to interview travel industry CEOs about their love of *Condé Nast Traveler* to be included in a video for the magazine's upcoming 15th Anniversary. The trip got off to a rough start in Singapore where customs officials confiscated my 15 packages of Dentyne—that amount of gum chewing was a crime in the notoriously strict country.

Later, the grand dame Raffles Hotel put on quite a show with an upgrade to the Presidential Suite that was so large it unnerved me—I had to close off entire wings in order not to get lost. I stripped down, donned a robe and escaped to the balcony thinking the heavy fragrant air might ease the jet lag.

A few minutes later, a private butler arriving with a tray of freshly carved exotic fruit interrupted my peace. This was the fifth act in a parade of VIP welcome gifts sprinkled about the suite including a tray of two-dozen handmade truffles, three bottles of chilled champagne, four types of organic cheese, and five servings of Singapore Slings. Evidently, the hotel's goal was to get me drunk and fat.

After delicately arranging the fruit explosion on the balcony, the butler retreated and closed the door behind him. I heard a click. I raced to the door, jiggled the handle, but nothing. I was locked out. Stuck on the balcony. My heart pounded. I pulled on the door desperately. No luck. The butler reappeared carrying a tray of six tubes of bath salts. Thank God. I waved furiously through the window. He smiled and waved back. I kept waving and shouting as he left the tray and exited the suite. Now I was panicked. I edged close to the balcony railing. I was three floors up, and if I swung out just right, I might be able to make it to the second floor without flashing anyone. As I gathered the robe through my legs, I felt a bulge. Thankfully, I had stashed my cell phone in the robe pocket, and dialed the front desk for a rescue.

The embarrassment only got worse on the next stop in my Asian immersion—Bangkok, the capital of sin. As was my norm, I had done mounds of advance research about gay spots and knew I wanted to journey to Babylon—a combo restaurant, bar, live entertainment venue, swimming pool, massage parlor, gay sex sauna, and more. Why should straights have all the fun in Pat Pong? After a full day of meetings, I returned to my gorgeous suite at the famed Oriental Hotel that once again came with a butler catering to my every whim. With the siren song of homo hedonism beckoning me, I stripped off my suit and tugged on a tank top ready for a wild night.

As I gently closed the door to my room, trying to sneak out of the hotel, my private butler magically appeared.

"Mr. Buchmeyer, like to use the house car tonight?"

"Um, no, that's fine, I'll just take a taxi."

"But Mr. Buchmeyer, general manager say take good care of you. Insist you use hotel car and driver."

"Really, that's okay. So generous. But a taxi is fine."

"Mr. Buchmeyer, no problem. Will call down and arrange car. Where you going?"

I was stuck. He stared, waiting.

"Just some club, I think it's called, let's see, um, Babylon."

I tried desperately to hide my shame. A wide grin came across his face.

"Mr. Buchmeyer going to Babylon! Crazy time at Babylon!"

As the elevator doors unfolded, the concierge yelled across the lobby.

"Mr. Buchmeyer, car is waiting to take you to Babylon! Right this way! Have fun at Babylon! Crazy place!"

I slinked through the lobby, and outside the bellboy shouted.

"This way, Mr. Buchmeyer, car to Babylon right here. You enjoy!"

The white stretch Mercedes limousine was conspicuous enough, but it was the shouting of my destination that mortified me. The driver greeted me.

"I hear Mr. Buchmeyer going to Babylon. Amazing place. You have much fun. I wait for you outside whenever you want to come home."

"Really, I can just get them to call me a taxi."

"No, general manager say must wait for Mr. Buchmeyer. No problem. Who knows? Mr. Buchmeyer may enjoy Babylon all night."

As the stretch limo pulled up in front of an enormous complex made to look like a French colonial plantation, the driver smiled.

"Babylon makes dreams come true!"

Inside, the labyrinth of gay sexual pleasure was a dream all right—like a porn movie imagined by Fellini. The famous shows in Pat Pong featuring women doing imaginative things with ping-pong balls in their vagina couldn't hold a candle to a Thai guy in a Viet Nam war sketch.

"G.I. Joe ice cold Coke bottle make me feel good. Like real thing!"

Repulsed, fascinated, and horny, I couldn't stop watching as the bottle magically disappeared into his ass. Ouch.

After many hours and several "massages" later, the Mercedes whisked me back to the opulent Oriental Hotel. Shame once again overcame me as I shuffled through the lobby at sunrise, and my private butler greeted me.

"I can see Mr. Buchmeyer enjoy Babylon. A lot."

My first meeting of the day was breakfast with the general manager of the hotel, an impeccably dressed German gentleman. He sipped his hot tea, examining my tired but dewy face glowing with satisfaction.

"You know, Mr. Buchmeyer, in a hotel, we watch your every move. Especially a VIP guest such as yourself from an important travel magazine."

I choked on my coffee.

"Not to worry, Mr. Buchmeyer. This is Bangkok. We've seen it all. Many times. If you weren't indulging, we would be worried. Now, for that hangover, perhaps you'd prefer an ice cold bottle of Coke?"

He smiled, and I relaxed. Editor was right—from Berlin to Bangkok I had quite a few adventures and collected many stories. But one thing I hadn't yet acquired was a boyfriend. The glamour of Babylon was fun once in awhile, but I was ready for something a little steadier.

Next on Alphabet City*:*

Jon Paul's search for a boyfriend goes better than expected. "I'm wondering about the well-endowed part."

Episode 14

Happy Soul

Jon Paul tries online dating and ends up revealing a hidden part of his past. Viewer Discretion Advised.

My hectic travel schedule left little time for dating story lines on *Alphabet City*. While I had a few recurring fan favorite boyfriend characters, including the Taxidermy Tax Attorney, there were no romantic episodes that were particularly earth shattering. A few years on the other side of 30, and the loneliness was wearing on me. While I was constantly forced into close proximity with a lot of eligible bachelors in this massively congested city, I just wasn't connecting with them on a level other than quickie sex. What little free time I had at home when not traveling, I didn't want to spend cruising for guys in a bar.

The Internet as hook up engine burst onto the gay scene in the late '90s. I signed up enthusiastically hoping that online matchmaking would prove superior to suggestive winks at seedy bars. Gay.com might expand my dating horizons, and so I fished in its online pond as NYCBUCKY.

My boyfriend search skills honed from years in gay bars were no help in cyberspace. It took several painful dinner first-dates to learn that chances were good the guy in real life will be the opposite of his description. DowntownHUNG was actually from the suburbs and had a widely inflated sense of his tool. STUDMuffin69 needed to lay off the pastries. 2Hard4U spoke about his dick non-stop—two hours of cock talk over noodles proved too hard for me.

Some guys would have given up on the online thing altogether. But I couldn't resist the Internet temptation—the gigantic desktop computer in my basement living room stared me down with the possibility that Mr. Right was right there waiting for my charming banter in the NYC chat room. The sound of static as the modem connected always sent a shiver of anticipation through me—Pavlov's gay dog. I scanned through the typical assortment of evocative screen names with requisite summary descriptions. There was always a "NYCockTop—8inches of meat, ready 2 pound U" and a "VillageDaddy—ready to spoil U and spank U."

One night, the screen name STARBSTRD caught my eye—nothing particularly sexual about that. Bastard? A little bit off putting really. Was that some kind of kinky sexual thing? But his description was tantalizing, endearing and funny: "Happy soul, well endowed." This STARBSTRD seemed different. I fretted over a good opening line for at least 30 seconds—an online eternity. He could be deeply involved with someone else by the time I finally messaged him.

NYCBUCKY: Are you a happy soul <u>because</u> you're well endowed?

Few second pause. No reply. I must have lost him. Then POP—a reply.

STARBSTRD: Funny ;-) I never connected the 2.

NYCBUCKY: Really? Most gay boys would!

And we were off. Over the course of the next 73 chat screens, I uncovered that he was:

30 years old—finally a boy my age!

Worked as an economist living on Wall St.—I'd never dated a banker!

From Mexico City—I loved Latinos!

Enjoyed dancing, food, yoga, rollerblading—I loved two of those things!

STARBSTRD: What's ur name?

NYCBUCKY: Jon Paul

STARBSTRD: That's funny!

Why was that funny? People making jokes about my name exhausted me. The next line was usually, "Oh, like John Paul Jones?" Or John Paul Sartre. Or John Paul George and Ringo. It's just one of those things I've heard my whole life and am prickly about. The chat had derailed and I was ready to end it over the name game.

STARBSTRD: Wanna come over and cuddle?

NYCBUCKY: Gimme a break.

Cuddle? What self-pronounced well-endowed gay guy thinks I'm going to believe that? Besides, if I did drag myself all the way to his apartment, I certainly hoped we would do more than just cuddle if his penis size lived up to proclamations.

STABRSTRD: Want to go on a date, then?

NYCBUCKY: Not really. I don't even know your name.

STARBSTRD: Juan Pablo.

NYCBUCKY: Not funny.

On the one hand, I gave him points for being clever—translating my name into Spanish. English Jon Paul became Spanish Juan Pablo. On the other, he had taken the name thing too far, and was living up to his screen name, acting like a bastard. I was tiring of this seemingly endless banter; it was hard to stay witty and disinterested at the same time. I was thinking of a nice way to shut down the chat, and then Pop Pop Pop—three screens in a row.

STARBSTRD: No, I'm not kidding.

STARBSTRD: We have the same name.

STARBSTRD: That's why I thought you were kidding.

What were the chances? Oh, the Internet. We had the same name—my Texas Jon Paul to his Mexican Juan Pablo. Of all the horny gay boy gin joint chat rooms in the world he had to log on to this one.

How could I not go out on a date with someone who had my same name? So I gave him my number and he phoned immediately to make plans for a date the next day. His voice was a surprise—no rolled "R's" or deep Latin baritone; instead his speech was slightly high pitched with an odd Pan-European accent we've come to associate with Madonna.

"If you could come downtown that would be great. Want to go rollerblading?" he asked.

I hated Wall Street, used Canal Street as the marker for my personal DMZ, and had only recently learned to roller blade. I imagined making a fool of myself splattering all over Battery Park.

"Blading doesn't seem like a first date kind of thing," I said.

"How about a stroll along the West Side?"

A stroll? He sounded positively Parisian, a flaneur. I was intrigued. In the hustle of New York City, I rarely just wandered aimlessly, but Happy Soul (well-endowed) sounded like he had a plan.

The next day, ten minutes before the appointed hour, I sat on a bench in the World Financial Center filled with Chinese brides in wedding dresses with bright pumps trailed by photographers. I was worried that I wouldn't recognize Juan Pablo from the picture he had emailed. He said it was of him on a recent trip to Thailand, which I expected would be him in a Speedo on a sandy beach. But the jpeg was a close shot of his sweaty smiling face next to a plate of glassy noodles with red peppers. What an odd choice. As his publicist, I'd counsel him to get a more flattering headshot.

"Hey Bucky, sorry, yoga ran long."

STARBSTRD was 15 minutes late, glistening from his workout. He was dressed in some last season baggy clam diggers from the GAP, an ill-fitting graphic t-shirt from French Connection, and an orange fisherman's hat from God knows where. I tried shaking off my snobby Condé Nast fashion sense.

"Oh hey, that's fine. I just got here, really," I lied.

I stood up and we smiled at each other, relieved that our real selves lived up to the online potential we advertised. As I looked past the clothes, he was handsome in an offbeat way, with brown eyes and an oversize nose punctuating a broad smile that bared his happy soul—think sweet face of Sean Astin with the sexy spirit of Gael Garcia Bernal. I was pretty charmed.

We hugged hello in that awkward way that comes when you have never met someone in person but nonetheless know a little too much about them—like their preference for top or bottom. He led me out the doors and onto the walking path. Even after five years, I had never ventured out of my cocoon and taken in the views of Lady Liberty and New Jersey from this side of the island.

Rollerbladers with no padding and no shirts displaying perfectly toned abs whizzed by us, dodging stuffed strollers and leashed dachshunds. I was glad I had resisted his initial offer of blading. There was no way I would have kept it together in this live action video game. But I was a little disappointed that he wasn't the darker skinned Latino that I imagined.

"You're whiter than I am. How are you from Mexico?" I blurted out.

"Thanks. I work at this color. My religion is sun block."

I laughed, not knowing if he was intentionally cracking a joke, or if English as a Second Language was going to be more of a problem—or benefit—than I bargained for. We strolled and chatted and teased about all the things you over-share on a first date in New York City—your job, your apartment, your previous life discarded to live in the center ring of the Big Apple circus.

"This is where I finally felt free to be myself, to explore," he said.

"Explore the museums?"

"Free to be gay. I was straight until I moved here."

That was a little unbelievable. It didn't take a finely honed Gaydar to tell either one of us had a thing for boys.

"I even had a girlfriend in London when I was in graduate school. I mean I thought I was attracted to guys. But I really knew when I moved to New York."

"What flipped the switch?"

"Dancing at Twilo."

"Really? You don't seem the type."

"There's all kinds there. I love to dance. My friends call me the Mexican Jumping Bean because I bounce!"

He did a little demonstration for me on the bike path, nearly knocking over one of those rollerblading Chelsea-boys I hated. The type that probably went to Twilo.

The famous far West Chelsea club was known as a den of hedonistic dancing and drug use. Having never been, I assumed Twilo was filled with the Chelsea boys I was so quick to deride on the street as all muscles and no brains; whose only interest was popping a pill and grinding against sweaty bodies on the dance floor. I had stayed away from those dance palaces, telling myself I didn't fit into the fraternity of chiseled looks, staying close to the smoky East Village bars filled with counter-culture homos. Juan Pablo continued telling me his sexual coming out story.

"When I first moved here, I'd go to Twilo every Friday with my straight friends. By the end of the night, I was always dancing with the shirtless guys on the dance floor, brushing up against them. Wishing I could go home with them. One night I did. I was so nervous. It was my first time with a guy."

I'd had enough "straight" men in health club steam rooms to know that curious guys let their peckers wander when opportunity knocks.

"You mean to tell me you've never had sex with a guy until recently? The whole time you lived in Europe, you never went in a gay sauna or video store and had sex?"

"Well, I walked by many of them. I always peeked in. But I just couldn't do it. Not while I had a girlfriend."

"I've never been able to pass up cheap European sex," I quipped.

"Hey, you want to get a bite to eat?" he asked.

I looked at my watch; we had been strolling for about two hours on a walk that should have taken twenty minutes. I felt something funny inside—a sense that this character, initially set-up as on online dating possibility, might become an important co-star in my life. Was I the Tex to his Mex?

"I thought you had some errands to do," I reminded him nervously.

"Well, I'd rather spend the day with you. Pastis is just around the corner, want to see if we can get in?"

My heart fluttered. Pastis had been in the gossip columns for months as the chic Meat Packing District hangout, but I had never been. My Condé Nast credentials were about to be revoked over this infraction. This guy may not have a fashion sense, but he had a bootie built for boogie and a fine-tuned restaurant radar. I could work with that.

After a quick walk, we settled into a table in the middle of the chaos of a restaurant that was trying too hard—too hard to pass off as a century old its newly created French bistro chic.

"I've been here several times and there are some things I want you to have. Do you mind if I just order for us?" Juan Pablo asked.

A little presumptive but taking charge. I liked that he wanted to share something, and used the word "us." This felt a little more intimate, a little more comfortable than your typical first date.

Within minutes, our table was filled plates of baby lettuce salads with goat cheese, bowls of frites and dozens of oysters. I loved that he didn't even ask if I was a fan of the slimy aphrodisiacs—because I would slurp them any which way to Friday. Surrounded by food, he looked like he was in heaven.

"Would you call yourself a foodie?" I asked.

"I guess I like food as much as the next guy. Don't you?"

"Maybe not as much as you. You took pictures of yourself all sweaty with those noodles in Thailand."

"Everyone takes pictures of food!"

"I've never once in my life taken a snapshot of my entrée."

"Well, you're missing out. And we're missing the aioli!"

He nearly tackled a disinterested waiter and insisted on a side of mayo for dipping. From my face he could tell I had never imagined anyone plunging fries into white whipped creamy sauce like that—everything else in Texas, yes—fried potatoes, crazy.

"I do it the French way," he declared.

I could have sworn I felt his sneaker brush up against my leg. The last time someone played footsie under the table with me I ended up with a job as a celebrity publicist battling the greasy advances of my boss. I encouragingly nudged back with my foot, and gave myself goose bumps.

"I just saw this hysterical John Waters' film called *Cecil B. DeMented*. Something about the guy in the film reminds me of you. The actor who plays the filmmaker in it—what's his name?"

"Stephen Dorff!" I shouted.

This was crazy. How in the world did Juan Pablo conjure up my celebrity doppelganger? The same one currently playing a two-bit independent filmmaker in the latest John Water's film? STARBRSTD was connecting to me in ways he couldn't possibly know about— unbeknownst to him he was carefully picking the lock on a part of my life I kept hidden from view. I tip toed into the shallow waters of revelation.

"That's funny. Well, the thing is, before I moved to New York City, I was an independent filmmaker."

"What do you mean? What kind of film?"

"It's called *GayTV: The Movie*—about a brother and sister who take over a bankrupt cable channel and launch their own television network called GayTV—All Gay, All Day. It's a big comedy with lots of parodies of TV shows like *GayE.R.* and *Charlie's Post-Op Angels*."

"Wow. How did I miss it?"

"You could have seen it at gay festivals in Torino or Philadelphia. Audiences loved it. But it never went anywhere."

I was quickly trying to bring the discussion to a close. Because the film never was distributed, the memories of what I often felt was an artistic failure ran deep—it was one of the reasons I ran away from Texas to the anonymity of New York. He nodded, enraptured by a story I didn't tell very often—because I was afraid of reactions like "he's a failure" and "why didn't he stick with it?" There was no judgment on his face—his eyes told a story of deep empathy like I had never experienced.

"That's why you moved to New York?"

"Partly. Life takes funny turns when you follow your dreams like that. My boyfriend left me. My sister who was my writing partner had a nervous breakdown. In the end, I was bankrupt, both emotionally and financially."

"But you must be so proud of what you created."

"I suppose. Proud that I picked myself up and moved on. After the movie, I saw myself in a different way. I realized that if I wanted to move to New York, I could do it. I'd made a movie for God sakes. I could do anything."

I took a deep breath. Glanced around nervously at the restaurant. Why did French bistros always scribble menus unintelligibly on broken chalkboards and moldy mirrors? I couldn't even name a French bistro in Dallas, but in New York City there was one on every corner.

He picked up his champagne glass and raised his mimosa.

"To you NYCBUCKY, and to the day I get to see *GayTV*!"

We clinked. I laughed, embarrassed that I just put so much of myself out there on the table, mixed in with the used oyster shells and last scraps of mayo.

"I don't know what you're doing this afternoon. But can I take you to see *Cecil B. Demented*?" he asked.

As we strolled from the just gentrifying sidewalks of the Meatpacking District down through the cobblestone streets of the West Village and across to the Angelika Film Center, we paid no attention to the outside world—completely consumed with each other. He quizzed me more about filmmaking. And I asked him more about coming out in his late-20s. He spoke slowly and deliberately, choosing every word as someone does who has learned English as his third language after French.

We settled into our seats in the darkened movie theater. Only a few die hard John Waters fans sprinkled the auditorium. The rumble of subway trains rattled the seats underneath adding unintended sensory feeling to the movie. I looked at Juan Pablo, and despite the noise distractions and the fact that he had seen this particular movie just days earlier, he was swept away by the film's cast of misfits including Melanie Griffith, Ricki Lake, and Mink Stole. When my Hollywood separated-at-birth twin Stephen Dorff appeared on screen, he smiled at me.

I reached out and held his hand. At first, he jerked slightly away, looked around, and then settled into it. We squeezed our hands tightly together for the rest of the movie, as if we were unwilling to let go of this moment, this date, this day.

After the film, we stood on a busy street corner in SoHo illuminated by the marquee and by our newfound feelings for each other. We were hesitant, unsure of how you end a date that began as a horny chat and ended—were we ready to admit it—in love.

"So this is so great. I don't really want it to end," he said, shuffling nervously.

"Me either. Is the offer still open to come over to your place?"

"I'd like that."

"Promise me something, though. I want a little more than just cuddling. I can see you're a happy soul. But I'm wondering about the well endowed part."

He hailed a cab right away. As the taxi crossed the DMZ of Canal Street, I held my breath until we pulled up outside a large building in the canyons of Wall Street—deserted and sinister looking. As if Batman might swoop down at any moment to save a damsel in distress.

Juan Pablo escorted me to the building's rooftop terrace where he produced a bottle of chilled Veuve Clicquot. The kid was smooth. We snuggled under the twinkling lights of skyscrapers and kissed deeply—in the city that doesn't sleep, I was about to be an insomniac. A few glasses later, and NYCBUCKY discovered STARBSTRD wasn't lying—well endowed, indeed.

Later, he spooned with me while I was trying desperately to keep still and not wiggle, to keep myself from doing what I always did after sleeping with a new guy—rushing home.

"What are you thinking about?" he asked

"It's been a long time since I've had a character this good on *Alphabet City*."

"I don't understand."

"You will. Welcome to the show."

Next on Alphabet City:

Jon Paul makes a tough decision about a trusted companion. "I can't put her through this anymore. I love her too much."

Episode 15

And Baby Makes Three

Jon Paul loses some of his closest friends; then gains some new ones.

There comes a time in every successful sitcom when new characters arrive and long-running storylines reach their conclusions. *Alphabet City's* season of transitions came in 2001. A few months after Juan Pablo became more than just an occasional guest star in my life, Angela announced that for work reasons she was moving back to Texas. The proclamation took me by surprise as I assumed that my longtime friend would always be by my side. After all, she was Phyllis to my Mary.

I organized an emotional send-off for Angela that included some star-studded cameos from Katie Couric and The Pope courtesy of a trip to the newly opened Madame Tussaud's Wax Museum in Times Square. Over a waxy wheelchair bound Christopher Reeves, Angela reassured me about her departure.

"You'll be fine. You've come a long way since we fought those Power Rangers to get that apartment. Now it's time to clear space for Juan Pablo," Angela said.

"It's a little early for us to even think about living together," I replied.

"Trust me, I can tell you two are meant for each other. Even Winnie likes him. And she's the most important one."

As usual, Angela was right. Soon after she moved out, Juan Pablo moved in as a permanent fixture on the *Alphabet City* set—much faster than I expected. The tragic events of 9/11 sent the city into a tailspin, and closed down Juan Pablo's apartment in Wall Street. The day after the tragedy, he and I hiked in a daze from the East Village to the tip of Manhattan to retrieve some of his personal effects. We waded through soot and debris, and weary first responders gave us surgical masks to limit our exposure to the toxic dust. We transported on our backs whatever clothes we could carry, and never looked back. In the aftermath of that cataclysmic event, we were glad to have each other, and Winnie was happy to have another companion in the house.

That Thanksgiving, as Juan Pablo and I got ready for bed after all our guests had departed, another character transition began. Winnie was acting abnormal—she was refusing to move from the couch and take up her spot in our bed. I was worried, and Juan Pablo tried calming my nerves.

"Maybe she's lethargic from eating too much turkey," he said.

"Who fed her turkey?"

"Everyone! She begs at the table constantly. You're overreacting."

"I'm her parent. I know when something's wrong."

The next day, I rushed Winnie to our trumpet playing Argentine vet Doc Moscovich—think facial expressions of Sid Caesar with the comic timing of Desi Arnaz. He laughed at my poultry suspicions.

"She's not sick from eating turkey! That's crazy. Where do you come up with these things?"

His mocking tone always calmed me. But I immediately tensed when he came and sat next to me. This was serious.

"I must tell you, Winnie is very sick. Her blood work shows she has a kidney problem."

"From eating chocolate?"

"No, no, no. It doesn't matter how. Now listen to me. The kidney problem will get worse. You can give her daily fluids. That will help for a while."

"What are you saying?"

"I'm saying that with the fluids, you'll have several more good months. You will know when it's her time."

My heart was pounding. I held a trembling Winnie close, hoping she wasn't listening. Doc Moscovich gave me a hug, and trained me to properly administer an IV with life saving saline solution. I decided to cancel my normal out-of-town holiday plans because the searing pain in my heart told me this would be the last time Winnie and I would ring in the New Year together.

Some time after Valentine's Day, after her infusion, Winnie was begging to go on a walk. She hadn't been so energized in months, and despite my concerns for her health, I couldn't refuse her request. I hooked on her harness and we stepped out onto the streets of the East Village.

As we walked, I remembered back six years earlier when Winnie and I had just arrived in the Big Apple. Her puppy tranquilizer drugs had worn off and she was begging to explore the mean streets of the East Village. I wasn't entirely sure how she would react to the sidewalks of the city. She was a foofy Texas dog through and through, used to open spaces and grass for peeing. I had no need to worry. That day, Winnie sassed her tail and acted like she was invited to every party along the street—the hipster card shop, Turkish pharmacy, Puerto Rican liquor store, and Korean Dry Cleaners.

Six years later, I realized we had been out for an hour and so far no pee. We ambled back towards our house, passing what was labeled a community garden, but looked more like an abandoned lot with junk piled high into a sculpture. Winnie sniffed her way up to the precarious exhibit—made from discarded stuffed animals, used furniture, Coke cans and Christmas ornaments. She bent her back legs and let it flow—adding her own yellow paint to the collective art installation. She looked back at me pleased with herself—it was the first smile from her in a long time. She had lived a good life, and left her mark on *Alphabet City*.

When we got home, I told Juan Pablo it was time.

"I can't put her through this anymore. I love her too much."

"And she loves you," he said.

"I just never knew it would be so soon. She's only 11. I assumed it would be years before I had to go through this. But I guess it's not fair any more. I need to let her go."

The last week of March, the three of us took our final journey together through the streets of the East Village. As I held Winnie close to my heart, she stared at me lovingly with her round black eyes and looked relieved. Doc Moscovich gave her one final shot. Juan Pablo hugged me as I rocked Winnie back and forth. She effortlessly slipped away—so peaceful and content.

"I love you little goose," I whispered.

"You're doing the right thing," Juan Pablo told me.

Saying goodbye to Winnie wounded my heart so deeply I wasn't sure I would recover. Just keep busy, I told myself. Keep moving. I told Juan Pablo that I needed to be by myself, and wandered the streets of Manhattan thinking about how much Winnie had touched my life. To date, she had been the longest relationship of my adult life, just barely edging out Angela, having acquired both of them in college. My heart felt empty where once her unconditional love had resided.

When I got home, Juan Pablo had packed away all of Winnie's effects, and I had to pack myself. I was leaving the next day for three weeks in Australia producing another television show for the magazine. The work was a welcome distraction from my grief. I reached in my nightstand for my sleeping pills and grabbed Winnie's puppy tranquilizers by mistake. She wouldn't need these anymore, but maybe I did.

***

A year later, after a rainy backyard memorial service for Winnie featuring a mail order statue of St. Francis that arrived beheaded, I was ready to welcome a bundle of love back into my life. I trolled the Internet, found a Bichon breeder in upstate New York and forged Juan Pablo's name on an adoption application.

I appreciated the breeder's sense of responsibility. From voluminous emails, I could tell this breeder's dog rearing philosophy was in sync with my own. Winnie had come from a pet store puppy mill, and God bless her, had life-long emotional scars to prove it. For our first child together, I thought Juan Pablo and I would do well with a more even-tempered dog. When we were approved with flying colors, I sprung the good news on Juan Pablo over dinner at our neighborhood bistro Le Tableau.

"So sweetie, I've been thinking that we're ready to have a family. To get another dog," I said.

"We? I'm not really a dog person," he replied.

"But you loved Winnie."

"I love you. And you came with Winnie. I had no choice."

"Okay. But as we build a life together, I think it's good for us to have a little one to raise. To share the joy of being Dads."

He pretty much knew there would be no way around this.

"I will do this for you. Because you want it. What's the process?"

"Well, that's the good news. We've already been approved. Can you believe it? We pick her up in a few weeks. Let's go home and I can show you pictures of her!"

Back at our apartment, I tried deflecting his questions about how long I had been plotting this by showing him online pictures of our newborn. The breeder did a masterful job of posing the puppies in front of objects to give a relative sense of their size. Ours was the runt of the litter, and Juan Pablo was astounded at her tiny body.

"She's smaller than that computer diskette! She's adorable!" Juan Pablo said.

My plan worked; he was hooked. One look is all it took to transform Juan Pablo into a doting dog father.

"Why do they call her yellow?" he asked.

"They call them colors instead of giving them a name. That's for us. What about naming her Charlotte, and calling her Charlie. Cute, right?"

"How about So-Shuh-Tuhl. Spelled X-O-C-H-T-I-L. It's the Mayan word for flower. Say it with me, Xochtil."

"You're kidding, right? I'm not naming her that. I can't even say it. I like Charlotte."

"What about Carlota? That's Charlotte in Spanish. Put Frida in front. Frida Carlota. Sounds like Frida Kahlo. And we could add Amarilla. That's yellow in Spanish."

"What's going on here? I thought you weren't a dog person."

"We'll call her Frida Carlota Xochtil Amarilla Buchmeyer Chavez!"

"What kind of fucked up name is that?"

"A true Mexican name! After all, she's going to be my daughter."

He puffed his chest out—all he needed was a cigar to complete the proud papa affect. Juan Pablo had won our first parenting argument. My plan had worked even better than expected.

Two weeks later, we packed into our powder blue Volkswagen convertible and motored upstate near Binghamton to collect our ward. I imagined rolling hills and a pastoral plantation of puppies frolicking in the grass. We were adopting a free-range Bichon Frise!

My bubble was burst when we pulled up in front of a ramshackle building with semi-detached doublewide. It couldn't possibly be the birthplace of our little girl. We must have made a wrong turn. But a crazy looking woman on the porch was waving at us—she had a tangled mess of curly hair and an apron embroidered with Bichons.

"Remember, we're in this together," Juan Pablo said.

Inside, we were surrounded by a whirlwind of puppy madness—canine mother, father, sons and daughter all racing about the dirty house like a tornado. Frida's birth breeder Debbie—think warm eyes of Sissy Spacek with the teased hair of Loretta Lynn—pointed at our little girl with a yellow bandana.

"Yellow put the 'run' in 'runt.' That's for sure. Gives her brothers a run for their money when the food comes out!" she yelled.

Frida wagged her microscopic tail at us and dribbled pee on what looked like once white shag carpeting. Debbie's crumbling bookcases were filled with every type of Bichon tzotchke imaginable—including such rare finds as Graduation Bichons in cap and gowns and Shaker Bichons featuring salt and pepper sprinkled out of the eye. Juan Pablo had an expression of sheer terror on his face. Unlike me, he hadn't been exposed much to the ways of Middle America living. This whole scene could have been played out in my mother's mobile home in East Texas.

Debbie reached down and picked up the little pup and handed her over to Juan Pablo. The runt laid flat on the palm of his hand and stared into his eyes. He smiled at her and I could tell they were in love.

We quickly paid our adoption fees, said our goodbyes, and Juan Pablo raced to the car with Frida in the palm of his hand. He propped her up on a special down pillow he had chosen and whispered in her ear.

"Don't worry, Frida Carlota. Your papas are here now. There's a Prada collar waiting for you at home!"

On the three-hour ride back to the city, I tried to prepare my co-parent for the many sleepless nights ahead.

"She's going to whine and cry, missing her family. I'm sure she'll hate her crate. Winnie did. But for proper potty training, we have to stick with it. I'm telling you, we're not getting any sleep for days. Just prepare yourself."

"You're awfully grim. I'm sure our Frida Carlota will be a dream," he said.

"Puppies are devious. She's snake charmed you already," I replied.

Once home, proud papa Juan Pablo carried his adopted charge across the threshold of the *Alphabet City* set and gently placed her on the floor. She looked around, sniffed, wagged her tail, and looked back at us panting with a huge grin. We had unpacked the box of Winnie's old items, thinking Frida might enjoy having a few things from her predecessor. She tottered over to examine some dog toys on the floor, and sunk her sharp puppy teeth into one of Winnie's favorites—an ugly orange rubber character with spikes of fake fur that we affectionately called Diarrhea Man.

Frida dragged the hideous toy inside the crate without any sign of hesitation. Then she promptly fell asleep. I was the one who couldn't rest all night, standing in the bedroom doorway, watching her tiny puppy breaths, marveling at her behavior.

"I just hope she doesn't miss her birth family too much," I said.

"Give me a break, with two Dads like us, that dog is never looking back."

Six months later, Frida got an even sweeter taste of the good life when Susan and I had to produce a red carpet event in Los Angeles for *Condé Nast Traveler*. All the main *Alphabet City* co-stars were out-of-town and I was stuck without a puppy-sitter.

"Let's just take her with us," Susan suggested.

"If anyone found out, I'd be fired."

"From Condé? Please. People here overnight their laptop to their hotel because it won't fit in their Louis Vuitton."

"At least they use the computer for work. I'm not sure you can say the same thing about a puppy."

"Then I'll make Frida stuff gift bags. Get over it. Celebrities travel with their dogs all the time. So can you. We're staying at the L'Ermitage, which is totally dog friendly. She'll have the time of her life."

Having run out of options, I phoned American Airlines and secured Frida a spot in the cabin with me. True to form, she slept through the flight like she'd been traveling trans-continental her entire life. Later, she settled into life at our Beverly Hills luxury hotel like a lord born to the manner. Ricky the Bellboy took her for walks at least four times a day. Blanca the Chamber Maid refused to service the room unless Frida was present. Samantha the Concierge indulged Frida's love of organic dog biscuits every time she pranced through the lobby. Celebrity publicist friends dropped off their pups for play dates at my suite.

Because she enjoyed herself so much on that first trip to Los Angeles, I let Frida tag along on all future trips to the West Coast. Every time I got out her traveling bag, she wagged her tail excitedly, climbed inside and fell right to sleep. One six-hour nap later, and she was prancing down Rodeo Drive.

One summer morning, Juan Pablo and I packed for a family getaway—just two dads in sandals and shorts with their precious daughter. When I got out Frida's carry bag, she wagged her tail and moved to get inside but stopped herself when she noticed Juan Pablo nearby. She was a creature of habit, and her Papa Juan Pablo was not part of the California routine.

She looked at us suspiciously. I nudged her inside and she reluctantly lay down, keeping close watch on the proceedings through her mesh window. A few hours later, I zipped open the bag to let her out. She had fallen asleep and was not interested in moving. She yawned and looked at me like I was crazy—we hadn't been traveling long enough for her usual in-flight nap. Juan Pablo tried coaxing her out.

"Come on Frida Carlota, you're going to love it here. Lots of dogs to play with. Other families with two Dads, just like us," he said.

We had come not to Frida's preferred Orange County but to Fire Island—a gay boy's beach oasis just a few hours by train from New York. Frida stepped tentatively out onto the boardwalk next to the ferry, looked around dazed and confused, sniffed the air and eyed me with a sneer. This certainly wasn't Beverly Hills. She turned around, stepped back inside her traveling crate, and lay down.

"Wow. We're raising a snob," Juan Pablo said.

"We? I thought you weren't a dog person?"

"When did I say that? I love our family!"

He kissed me on the cheek. A little bark came from the crate. Frida had reconsidered. She was ready for a walk around the island with her proud papas after all.

Next on Alphabet City:

Jon Paul's South Africa photo shoot turns dangerous. "Any sudden moves and it could be over in a manner of minutes."

Episode 16

Boots

Jon Paul's glamorous life of luxury travel comes to a halt thanks to a celebrity. Guest Star: Ashley Judd.

The white chateau glistening at the base of South Africa's lush green mountains was exactly the type of stunning setting I had come to expect from a *Condé Nast Traveler* cover. Once again, I was on hand to make sure everything ran smoothly for the photo shoot having proved over the past six years that I was more than just a publicist. Whether it was prying beauty secrets from Paloma Picasso and scoring a private tour of her father's collection at the Tate Gallery, or cajoling Wayne Newton into opening up his private Vegas showplace and hosting the magazine's awards show, I was often the publication's go-to fixer.

But the stakes were even higher on this trip to Cape Town—I was entrusted to secure a crucial cover for the September All-Star issue. It seemed so simple a few months ago in New York when I pitched the concept and made a few calls. But on the ground in South Africa, things had been getting complicated and emotional. Just this morning, while taking in the extreme poverty of the city's infamous Khayelitsha Township, a six year-old orphan boy had peed on me. And now, I was throwing rocks at one-of-a-kind Hermès riding boots in an effort to make them look "authentic" for the luxury shoot. The Dutch photographer inserted a late change to the set-up that made me even more nervous—an additional model, whose handler had just arrived dressed as a safari ranger. He pointed at me, the photographer, and model.

"Only three of you are approved to be on the set. Any sudden moves and it could be over in a matter of minutes," he warned.

I winced, worried that I had been slamming back coffee all day and was a little too jittery. Our famous female model peeked inside the van at her caged co-star and grinned.

"I've always dreamed of working with a leopard!" she shouted.

I smiled back out of sheer terror—it was entirely plausible that our cover subject, actor and activist Ashley Judd, could be fatally injured on my watch. It was not the ending I had in mind after a half-dozen years, 22 exotic countries, 21 original television shows, and nearly one million frequent flier miles.

A few months earlier, Editor convened a meeting with me and several editors about finding a celebrity for the cover of its All-Star issue. Celebrity publicists had been turning down the magazine's cover offers right and left, and Editor wanted us to find a solution. I suggested an idea to make the process easier: honor an A-Lister for their charity work.

"How is that going to help us?" Editor asked.

"Publicists are saying 'no' to you because they have no reason to say 'yes.' They'd rather their clients be on the cover of *Vanity Fair* to promote their project," I said.

I felt like I was leading a graduate seminar titled Famous Faces & Flacks: Understanding Motivation.

"But I bet if we found a charity with a celebrity supporter, things would be different. Charities want the visibility with our wealthy readers, so they have a vested interest in delivering their spokesperson. Go through the charity, not the celebrity publicist."

"Alright, we're running out of options. Try it," Editor announced.

One quick call to the savvy leader of YouthAIDS Kate Roberts and a deal was struck to follow their spokesperson Ashley Judd. She had an upcoming trip planned to South Africa visiting the group's programs working to end HIV transmission in children. Editor dispatched me to Cape Town to make sure everything went according to plan.

A few minutes after I checked in to the luxurious Cape Grace Hotel at the base of Table Mountain, I was summoned to Ashley's suite for an advance meeting about our tour of AIDS clinics and orphanages the next day. The YouthAIDS team had just arrived from Mozambique where Ashley had slept on the floor of mud huts with commercial sex workers in order to better understand their plight.

In Ashley's room, the organization's South African staff was assembled around a large dining room table. Ashley was all business, scribbling notes on the facts and figures flying about. I was immediately impressed by her grasp of cultural taboos that sometimes complicated effective harm reduction programs. She framed hard-hitting questions about government inaction and asked for updated disease transmission statistics that she would need for a series of press interviews. Then, Ashley effortlessly shifted her attention away from the intricacies of a global pandemic to the delicacies of a magazine cover shoot.

"Now JP, I'd like to go through the clothes for the shoot," she said.

We moved to the suite's living room where she scanned through racks of high-end attire, and trained her eye on a fabulous pair of knee-high leather boots.

"These are going to need to be scuffed or it won't look right. That won't be a problem will it JP?" she asked.

"We can fix it. But I have to ask. Doesn't this photo shoot seem so much less important than the AIDS work?"

"For me, it's not one or the other. If I can use my fame to draw attention to the crisis, then I've done my job. Tomorrow's going to be a tough day. You better get some sleep."

Ashley gave me a hug and sent me off to bed. The next morning, a crowd of photographers followed Ashley and entourage through clinic tours, testing sites, peer education programs, and a lunch with female hairdressers who were using their salons as distribution centers for safe sex messages. At every turn, Ashley was poised, and able to effortlessly answer any question about the epidemic.

Early afternoon, we piled into a caravan of black SUVs and traded the flashbulbs and admiring crowds of Cape Town for the filthy streets and dying orphans of AIDS ravaged Khayelitsha Township. While I had seen much poverty around the world, I was ill prepared for the devastation from the epidemic I witnessed at Ashley's side. She took me by the hand, lead me into a hospital treating dying children, and taught me to sit at the bedside of a 15-year old who was so emaciated from AIDS that he looked ten. She showed me how to run my fingertips lightly along his arm.

"Stroke like this. Everyone needs a human touch."

We moved from bedside to bedside of these abandoned and dying children for over an hour. Ashley looked up at me every so often and smiled, encouraging me to keep giving and touching despite the heart-breaking situation. I'd never seen such a caring and committed celebrity.

At one point, a six-year old boy with AIDS sporting yellow rain boots sat in my lap and demanded I carry him with me around the ward. We nicknamed him Boots, and as I was about to leave, he couldn't control his bladder and peed all over me. I just smiled and kissed his forehead as I laid him back down in his bed.

Later that day, my mind was a mess by the time the SUVs pulled up outside the chateau for the cover shoot. I tried shaking off the horror I had witnessed earlier to focus on capturing an image that would sell magazines, but it all seemed so pointless. I knocked on Ashley's trailer and handed over the roughed up Hermès boots.

"How do you not feel guilty about all this luxury?" I asked.

"Remember, it's never a choice, JP. Never feel guilty for what you have. Not as long as you work so that others have access to what they need. It's never a choice."

She'd thought a lot about this disparity. Ashley strapped on the boots and fluffed her hair.

"Now where's that leopard? That's a shot that will sell!"

Ashley was a woman on a mission who trained her laser-like attention on a problem and attacked it with vigor. Opinionated, she rarely suffered fools gladly—something that often rubbed people the wrong way, similar to other pop-culture crusaders like Madonna or Angelina. But seeing her in both spheres—the glamorous and the destitute—I appreciated the veneer she used like a passport to travel between the first and third worlds.

When my plane touched down in New York, I entered a new era. My boss had been promoted to creative director for the company. That meant that Editor and I would no longer work side-by-side, traveling the globe. And a call from the YouthAIDS team confirmed my worry—just after I left Cape Town, Boots had died. I might have been the last person to hold him, touch him, and kiss him.

The South Africa experience felt like the dramatic cap to a critical story arc for my character. In what seemed like a blink of an eye—but in real time had been six years—I had traveled the globe with an engaging cast of characters, and journeyed inside myself awakening a definite confidence, adventurous spirit, and reservoir of deep emotions.

Condé Nast was like a finishing school for the kid from Texas—I had gone from naïve newbie to savvy insider with a renewed belief that my determination would take me far. But after a million miles, I needed a break from all the take-offs and landings. I needed time to regroup and focus on what might lay ahead for the star of *Alphabet City*.

Next on Alphabet City*:*

Jon Paul takes on a new challenge. "My biological clock is ticking!"

Episode 17

Turn the World on With A Smile

After ten years, Jon Paul becomes a true New Yorker. The streetlights dim on Alphabet City. Series Finale.

The rhythmic pulse of river water rushing over stones near the rice paddies was the most therapeutic sound I had heard in years. Now I understood why travelers found this spot so mythic. Because of a Rogers and Hammerstein melody that had haunted me as a kid, I had flown half way around the globe to the island paradise of Bali.

As the sky turned a comforting burnt orange, three stooped field workers planted their last grains of rice and pulled their cart off stage. They must be actors hired to complete this perfect tableau, part of a Four Seasons theme park ride. This calm was exactly what had I been searching for when I decided to take a hiatus from the pressures of Condé Nast. Interrupting my moment of peace was my dear friend Dana—think bravada of Princess Leia with the style of Maggie Gyllenhaal.

"It's time for you to grow up and buy real estate," she said.

Dana addressed me from her lounge chair by the infinity pool of our chic riverside suite at the Four Seasons Sayan, the latest in a series of romantic destinations we had visited together. One of my duties at *Condé Nast Traveler* had been producing the magazine's television shows, and as senior editor, Dana was the host. Traveling like a married couple from the South of France to Rio de Janeiro, we learned to cope with each other's traveling antics. I discovered that Dana had a fear of dehydration and a sugar addiction, so I kept us stocked in bottles of water and bags of gummy bears. She learned that I had bouts of seasickness and a lowbrow reading addiction, so she kept on-hand a supply of Dramamine and celebrity biographies. I was astonished by her uncanny ability to lose her government issued photo i.d. between check-in and security. She was irritated by my quirk of always sneezing exactly three times.

Dana was the only person I knew who would jet halfway round the world for less than a week of vacation. She did so willingly, sensing I was at a crossroads. She was there to record it in watercolors; her brushes and painters notebook spread out in front of her.

"Face it, I'm from Florida and you're from Texas, owning a house is just in our blood," Dana said.

She knew I delighted in her references to our shared white trash roots. She smeared a bright orange line across the blank page she was holding in her lap. I raised myself out of the warm water and lay next to her on the doublewide lounge chair.

"I don't know. Buying in New York is so complicated. I don't think I'm ready," I said.

"Ready? No one's ever ready. Quit making excuses. You just don't want to commit."

"I'm not afraid to commit. Juan Pablo and I have been together almost six years now."

"Tex, you're afraid to commit to New York. You need to create a home for yourself."

Dana understood the importance of home for me. We both had been uprooted and moved about much of our childhoods, and ultimately escaped to New York to live a dream. I admired her spirit and attitude. In the short space of a couple of years, she had become a real estate maven having purchased two apartments—trading one in with a discarded relationship. In terms of owning property, she knew what she was talking about.

"Maybe you're right. But I don't even know where to start."

"Get yourself a copy of *Real Estate for Dummies* and you'll be in business," she said.

Dana chose a bright red color and painted a baseball cap on my figure on her canvas. In triumph, she handed over a still drying memento of me laying poolside in Bali. The little painting captured perfectly a turning point in my life.

A week later in late May, Real Estate Tsunami JP hit the East Village set of *Alphabet City*—a torrent of anticipation upgraded from a tropical storm of excitement and jet lag. I scurried about scooping up bank statements, tax forms, everything we would need for a possible date with a mortgage broker.

"You're manic. What's all this about?" Juan Pablo asked.

"It's time to grow up. My biological clock is ticking."

"You want a kid?"

"No, a house!"

There was no arguing with me once I put my mind to it. And Juan Pablo didn't dislike the idea—a trained economist, he had been preaching to me the long-term investment strategy of owning property. I didn't care about the financial aspects; I yearned for the stability. I had arrived in New York City looking for an adventure, and had found it. I couldn't imagine ever leaving the city—once an outsider, now I belonged here. And I wanted a home that went along with that sense of entitlement.

Of course, I would have been perfectly content to stay in the East Village if there was a reasonably priced set available. The neighborhood had grown up alongside me, and I liked to the think that the area had officially arrived partly due to the popularity of *Alphabet City*. Property values were skyrocketing and that meant owning an equivalent apartment in the area was out of the question.

Over the next two days, I began pouring over online listings for brownstones in our price range. We had decided that we wanted to avoid the intrusiveness of New York's notorious co-op boards by purchasing a small building. In short order, I gave the once-over to 19 different properties all over the city.

For what we could afford, Harlem was already too pricey. For our limited price range, most Brooklyn neighborhoods were still too sketchy. But something intrigued me in a neighborhood I had never even considered, Washington Heights—perched precariously at the tip of the island of Manhattan. The 'hood was infamous as the cocaine capital of the city during the '80s, but I read that the area had cleaned up its act with the influx of artists and young couples priced out of Harlem just to the south. That sounded like us!

The newest wave of gentrification enthusiasts were just the latest in a long line of immigrants that included Poles, Greeks, Irish and Jews, who founded Yeshiva University nearby. Now the Dominicans lived in easy rhythm with the Orthodox—they drove the gypsy cabs, ran the kosher-friendly grocery store, and held the doors to temple on Sabbath. The A-train subway platforms were packed with a mix of dark-skinned JLo's who were scantily clad in hip hugging jeans next to pale-faced Rachel's who were completely covered in headscarves and wigs.

Real Estate for Dummies was a reliable guide to the mysterious language of property transactions. But what it didn't prepare me for was the emotional reaction I had when I saw a thin 4-story brownstone struggling to stand tall on sloping 183rd street. I knew in my heart I had not only found the new set for my sitcom life, I had found a home. I dragged Juan Pablo to see the building.

"How can you know this is it? We need to see more places," he said.

"Wait until you see inside. You'll know. Don't you think the outside has potential? I'm seeing flower boxes and a new front porch light."

Our head-to-toe tattooed real estate agent Chuck moonlighted as Dana's boyfriend, and met us at the door stubbing out one of the cigarettes he was chain smoking. He battered us like a music-industry dealmaker—think voice of Howard Stern with the spirit of Hans Solo.

"This is the place guys. This is the place. This is it. But you gotta act fast. Not many places like this around. It'll go fast."

"Chuck, the place has been on the market for three months," I said.

"Look at this stove! It's huge. It looks industrial," Juan Pablo yelled.

"It's from a restaurant. The previous owner got it at a close-out sale," Chuck said.

"Isn't it illegal to have commercial grade appliances in a residential building?" Juan Pablo asked.

"Who's gonna know?"

"The police officers at the precinct on the end of the block," Juan Pablo replied.

"You guys wander around. I'll be outside smoking."

As Chuck retreated, we climbed the wooden stairs for a floor-by-floor inspection, noting things that would need simple fixes like repainting the hallways' custard yellow walls and replacing the bedrooms' 70s track lighting. The space worked perfectly for a French farce and sitcom life: first floor chef's kitchen and dining room for entertaining; second floor guest bedrooms and home offices; third floor living quarters; and a spacious fourth floor one-bedroom apartment for potential new guest stars.

I insisted on seeing the roof of the building. It's what you would do in Texas. But as always, things were a little more complicated in the Big Apple. In order to ascend to the top of the building, I had to climb out of the fourth floor window and immediately onto a ladder whose rusty hinges looked far from stable. Juan Pablo and Chuck were having none of it, so the final inspection was up to me. I was dressed more for yachting than inspecting—outfitted in summer linen trousers and Fendi flip-flops. I popped out the window, and exhaled quickly as I grasped the metal ladder and raced up the rungs, never looking down.

"Bombs away!" I yelled.

Once on the roof, I quickly sprinted to the middle, nervous that my slight phobia of heights was about to rear its ugly head. I soaked in the view of the neighborhood—the white spire of the nearby Baptist church, the medieval towers of The Cloisters peeking through Ft. Tryon's trees, and the movie theater marquee on 181st street.

Pinned to the outside of the film center's wall was a giant poster for the charming documentary *Mad Hot Ballroom*. I smiled remembering the triumphant story of the dancing crazed neighborhood kids. I imitated the pre-teen Dominican stars on the poster—I spun around like Mary Richards. But I stopped suddenly, nearly falling over. My sandals were stuck to the summer heated tar on the building's rooftop.

Later, I regrouped with Juan Pablo in the building's Mexican tiled outdoor patio garden with built-in fireplace.

"We'll call this spot Frida's garden. You're right. It's perfect," Juan Pablo said.

"Remember the story of the Japanese Power Rangers? I never thought I'd find another place as wonderful," I replied.

We decided to make an offer right away. Within weeks we were battling various villains involved in New York real estate transactions including Lazy Lawyers and Draining Deposits. But soon enough, we owned a tiny piece of the island of Manhattan. And just as quickly our East Village living room was filled with packing tape, unmade boxes and white tissue paper for the breakables—transferring the *Alphabet City* set was a monumental undertaking.

One morning, little Frida eyed me suspiciously from her perch on the red sectional couch. I was frantically searching for the ringing phone, and found it inside a box of framed pictures from my childhood. From the caller i.d., I knew it was my Texas friend Jimmy.

"Hey there. Today's *Dallas Morning News* says your Dad was found wandering around outside his house, in the middle of the night, with no pants. The police found open liquor bottles and lots of pills in the house," Jimmy said.

I sighed and shook my head, out of frustration, not surprise. I was irritated that the life I was so desperately trying to leave behind in Texas had once again intruded on my New York existence. I worked hard at keeping a carefully calibrated distance from my family in Dallas, choosing to build my own support structure up North. I traveled the world rather than go home for the holidays. Reminded myself that I left behind pain when I exited the Lone Star state. Convinced myself that the years of therapy as a teenager had healed forever the wounds of a childhood filled with abandonment.

But every so often, something tugged at my familial puppet strings that forced me into the role of dutiful son to a powerful father. Once again, I felt obligated to live up to society's expectations, and behave like a caring family member. I hung up with Jimmy, and flew to Texas to my father's bedside.

At Dallas' sprawling Baylor Hospital, the collected Buchmeyer children—two sisters, my half-brother and me—were like broken dolls returned to the factory of our birth. The confident young doctor explained my father's illness.

"Your father doesn't have Alzheimer's, he has vascular dementia. It's brought on by his strokes. For this episode, we think your father overdosed on his medications because he couldn't remember which ones he'd already taken. He had everything from sleeping pills to muscle relaxers to alcohol in his system."

I wasn't surprised. Those were his addictions.

"We're going to keep him here for several days. I won't lie. It's going to be rough. He'll be going through detox. But the funny thing with dementia is that if there's no alcohol around, he won't remember to drink."

Funny, I wish I could get dementia of the soul and not remember parts of my past.

"Please understand, his memory won't get any better. You'll need to make plans for him to stop working."

I couldn't see that happening. My father's entire life was work. He was alone after three failed marriages and now just lived for the courthouse. Stop the work and kill the man.

"He'll pretty need much constant care. It's good to have his whole family here."

Whole family? Could the doctor not feel the sickening tension in my father's private hospital room? My two sisters had fought all their lives and now only barely tolerated each other. I hadn't spoken to my oldest sibling in years after our movie venture. Now, she could hardly even look at me. It wasn't clear if my half-brother could function when he wasn't in rehab or getting another tattoo. None of us had a particularly close relationship with my father to begin with, but my own was emotionally abusive. It's good to have the "whole" family here, indeed.

"Oh, and I almost forgot. Because of your father's high profile, we tried to keep his identity secret. But word leaked out about his condition, and now the press is calling. One of you will need to serve as a spokesperson and issue a statement."

I smiled at the absurdity of it, and then I switched on public relations autopilot. I reached into my bag, pulled out a notebook and began outlining a statement. If my years as a publicist in New York were good for anything, they taught me how to put on a brave face in a crisis.

A few days later, I left the press calls of Dallas behind. My plane to New York banked a hard left after Newark and headed up the Hudson River. I took in the majestic view of Manhattan below. My interest in the skyline normally petered out somewhere around Central Park—I was a downtown boy and found the Upper West Side too stroller-friendly for my tastes. But this time it was different—as we neared the George Washington Bridge, I pressed my nose to the glass and got a chill. I owned an entire lot on the most expensive island in America. This was the first time I returned from a trip and didn't just think, "I live there." This time, I was thinking, "I'm home."

Back on the East Village set of *Alphabet City*, I raced down the stairs, past the stacks of moving boxes, and into my windowless bedroom that was as dark and as cold as a cave. I pulled the covers under my chin, tugged lazy little Frida close, told Juan Pablo I didn't want dinner, and went to sleep.

I didn't get out of bed for two days. There were moments when I knew it was important for me to at least shower or move to the couch, and possibly pack a few boxes. But my mental concentration was not strong enough to summon action from my body. I reasoned that the trip had taken so much out of me. I was getting sick. I needed rest.

Juan Pablo came and lay next to me and stroked my head. He convinced Frida that she needed to go outside to pee, and then returned her to my side. After three days of watching me take to my bed like a Southern damsel, his indulgence turned to concern. He spoke to me the way you do to someone you are not sure is dealing with a full deck.

"I'm worried about you," he said.

"Me too. I'm sinking like a rock to the bottom. I know this feeling. I need help."

"What can I do?" he asked.

"I'm not sure you can do anything."

"I don't want you feeling like this, sweetie."

I managed a small smile. He had picked up "sweetie" from me, using it not in the Southern-too-familiar-way, and not in the Yankee-slightly-judgmental-way, but with his own warm Latino-English-as-a-second-language-loving way.

"I need to talk to someone about it," I said.

The next day I called Dana for advice. She'd had a tough time of it over the years, including a stint in rehab, but had come out the other side with an acerbic wit and off-beat fashion flare all her own. Some found her self-actualization abrasive, but I found it refreshing. I wanted some of that. When I told her I had sunk into a depression and needed a life line she screamed.

"Oh my God! I'm thrilled. Of course, you must go see my Ann. She's amazing, and she'll be tough on you—and that's exactly what a big personality like you needs."

"Thanks. Is that a compliment?"

"I mean you need someone who won't let you get away with anything. Who will call you on all your shit. Make you deal with your fucked up family in Texas. It's going to be great."

"You're acting like I just told you I'm pregnant."

"This is bigger. You're going to start therapy! In New York! Don't you know what that means?"

"That I'm totally screwed up?"

"In New York, therapy is a right of passage, honey. Welcome to the club, Tex. You've arrived. You're a true New Yorker!"

Over the next few weeks, I began seeing Dana's therapist. Because of my early childhood '70s TV obsession, I pictured her as a female Bob Newhart. Meanwhile, friends and supporting cast members of *Alphabet City* pitched in to pack up ten years worth of set decorations. It only took two hours for the cute gang of Polish movers to load it all into several large moving vans.

I stood staring at the blank walls and echoing space, holding Frida tight, fingering the apartment keys that John the Greek Landlord had trusted me with ten years ago. Juan Pablo gave me a little hug.

"You okay?"

"Yeah, just sad. *Alphabet City* had a good run here, you know?"

My mind raced through a montage of audience favorites—Whoopi and the Oscar, Tyra and the Turkish Rug, Graham Norton and The Ferret.

"I just don't know what to call it anymore," I said.

"Call what?"

"My sitcom life. Moving to the barrio feels like *Alphabet City's* been sent to another network. But I don't know which one."

"Telemundo?"

I tossed the idea around in my head.

"A character in a Spanish tele-novella, huh? I think I can work with that."

Alphabet City had run its course on the network of streets in the East Village. The plucky gay boy Mary Tyler Moore had come so far, no longer the new kid in town. In ten years, I transformed from struggling to successful, single to partnered. No longer ignoring my tortured past, but facing it with some much needed psychotherapy. I was here to stay, but determined to keep my Texas bred optimistic attitude while embracing all that New York still had left to teach. Just like Mary, I knew that whatever I did, I could turn the world on with a smile.

Juan Pablo held open the door as I placed the keys on the kitchen counter and turned out the lights on *Alphabet City*.

Episode 18

Acknowledgments

Jon Paul imagines his thank-you moment as an Oscar acceptance speech.

Oh my goodness. So many people to thank for getting me to this place. Wow, this thing is heavy! Okay, I've got to hurry up. I've made a list, so bare with me. And don't try to cut me off with the music. This is my moment. Okay, here goes.

Susan, you're the best friend—and business partner—a guy could ever have. Sensacional! Get 'em, get 'em.

Paige, the sisterly love, support, and edits mean the world to me. Thank God you whipped into shape my overuse of commas!

Dana, you believed in me from the beginning, gave me a shot and encouragement, and a life-saving referral.

Angela, thanks for not being Grace to my Will.

Shannon, you bring such sunshine to my life. Thank you for being pure joy.

Jimmy, you laugh in all the right places. "I'm thinking…lunch."

Aaron, your incisive comments were just what I needed.

Cleigh, you are truly my uncle. Thanks for opening your home—and arms—to me.

Dr. Ann, our work helped me open up, making this book much better.

To my writing teachers, Ana Maria Spagna and Kyle Minor, your positive critiques showed me the way.

Sam, your visual touch is tremendous.

To my amazing supporting characters, especially Publisher and Editor, thank you for teaching me so much about life.

Wait is that the music? Am I out of time? Oh, no. One more. The most important.

To my partner Juan Pablo, thank you for tolerating my antics, suffering my obsessions and encouraging my dreams. You are indeed exactly as advertised—happy soul and all.

Now, just rest Frida!

About the Author

After a successful run as the engaging star of *Alphabet City*, Jon Paul Buchmeyer moved to WaHi—the Washington Heights neighborhood of Manhattan. Currently, he is developing a new sitcom for the next season of his life called *40, Love*.

Jon Paul's writing has appeared in *Condé Nast Traveler* and *Bon Appétit*. Before moving to New York City, he was an independent filmmaker, directing a feature comedy called *GayTV: The Movie*. The film played to standing room only crowds at gay film festivals as glamorous and far-flung as Turin, Italy and Philadelphia, Pennsylvania.

ABCityblog.com features more of Jon Paul's writing, film clips, and behind-the-scenes stories and images of *Alphabet City*.

www.ingramcontent.com/pod-product-compliance
Lightning Source LLC
LaVergne TN
LVHW011421080426
835512LV00005B/197